Piano Hymns FOR DUMMIES®

**Performance Notes by Mary Ellen Pethel
and Stan Pethel**

D1597060

ISBN: 978-1-4234-7389-3

HAL•LEONARD® CORPORATION

7777 W. BLUEMOUND RD. P.O. BOX 13819 MILWAUKEE, WI 53213

Visit Hal Leonard Online at
www.halleonard.com

Table of Contents

Introduction

· ·

The 65 tunes included in this volume span a time period from the early years of the Christian church to more modern times. We include songs with strong and stately texts and tunes with complex harmonies, as well as simple repetitive choruses with straightforward chords. Each one has a unique place in the body of songs known and loved in the Christian faith.

The term "hymn" has it origins in the Greek word *hymnos,* which means "song or ode in praise of gods or heroes." It is used in *Septuagint,* which is the Greek translation of the Hebrew Bible, for various words meaning "song praising God." Over the years, the term has broadened widely to represent almost any song appropriately used in worship, either corporate or private.

Although formal hymnody may not recognize some of the spirituals, choruses, gospel, and folk songs that are included in this collection, the general public accepts these songs as hymns.

About This Book

The music in this book is presented in a *three-staff layout.* The vocal line is on top with the lyrics and a two-line accompaniment below it. The two-line accompaniment is often called a *Grand Staff,* because it has both treble and bass clefs that are played by one person.

You can accompany yourself, a soloist, or a group by playing the accompaniment, but the "piano part" includes the melody of the song, so you can use it as an instrumental solo as well. A violin or flute can play the melody as it is written. The melody would be the top notes in the treble clef.

Most of the songs are in what we call *friendly* keys. That means they don't have a lot of heavy key signatures, but are in the good piano keys such as C major with no sharps or flats, F major with one flat, or G major with one sharp. Some songs are in E♭ major with three flats and D major with two sharps, but those are manageable.

As with any musical activity, the more you practice and play, the better you will become in performing these great tunes. Hymns are great for group singing, and it seems there is always a need for people with the skills of hymn playing and hymn leadership. These songs are a great starting point.

How to Use This Book

Each song in this book has a unique history in its creation and use, so first you will find something about the lyricist, the composer, the time in which it was created, or how it relates to other songs and its time period. Following each hymn's history are some performance suggestions. Included are tips on making the performance more interesting by adding an introduction, creating an ending, simplifying the playing demands, as well as some instructions regarding the layout or form of the song.

More advanced players will know how to do these kinds of things already, but those with less experience can gain from the ideas presented. Use what you can and feel free to apply performance tips from one song to another if they suit your purposes.

Glossary

Music has its own special language. Here are some of the terms we use in this book:

✔ **Agogic:** This is an accent that occurs naturally on the beat.

✔ *Allargando:* Slowing down and getting louder, usually at the end of a song.

✔ *Arpeggio:* A broken chord played one note at a time, usually bottom to top.

✔ **Cadence:** The last two chords of a musical phrase or statement.

✔ *Fermata:* Holding out a note and stopping the rhythm.

✔ **Modulation:** Changing the tonal center, usually the key signature as well.

✔ *Morendo:* Gradually dying away in volume.

✔ *Ritard:* A gradual slowing of the tempo.

✔ *Siciliana:* A song with a rocking feel in 6/8, like a swaying boat.

✔ **Shuffle:** A performance practice using *swing eighths*.

✔ **Straight eighths:** Divide the beat into two equal parts.

✔ **Swing eighths:** Divide the beat into three parts, with what is called a *triplet feel.* The first note in the beat will be longer than the last note.

✔ *Tessitura:* The general range of a melody.

✔ **Vamp:** A repeated passage, usually with a bass line and simple chords.

Icons Used in This Book

In the margins of this book are several handy icons to help make following the performance notes easier:

A reason to stop and review advice that can prevent personal injury from happening to your fingers, your brain, or your ego.

These are optional parts, or alternate approaches that those who'd like to find their way through the song with a distinctive flair can take. Often these are slightly more challenging routes, but encouraged nonetheless. There's nothing like a good challenge!

This is where you will find notes about specific musical concepts that are relevant but confusing to just about every non-musical type — stuff that you wouldn't bring up, say, at a frat party or at your kid's soccer game.

You get lots of these tips, because the more playing suggestions we can offer, the better you'll play. And isn't that what it's all about?

About the Authors

The writers of *Piano Hymns For Dummies* are a father/daughter writing team. **Mary Ellen Pethel** wrote the histories and background of the hymns. She is a history teacher at both the high school and college level, currently teaching at Harpeth Hall School in Nashville, Tennessee. She holds a Ph.D. in history from Georgia State University, a Master of Education from Berry College, and a Bachelor of Arts in history from the University of Tennessee.

Stan Pethel wrote the introductory materials and the performance tips. He is the Chair of Fine Arts at Berry College in Rome, Georgia, as well as a recognized composer and arranger of music. Prior to his position at Berry College he was a Middle School Band Director in Clarke County, Georgia. He holds a Doctor of Musical Arts from the University of Kentucky, a Master of Fine Arts in music composition, and a Bachelor of Music in Education from the University of Georgia.

Amazing Grace

Words by John Newton
Traditional American Melody

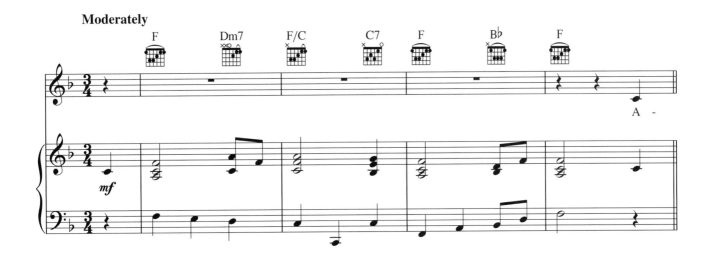

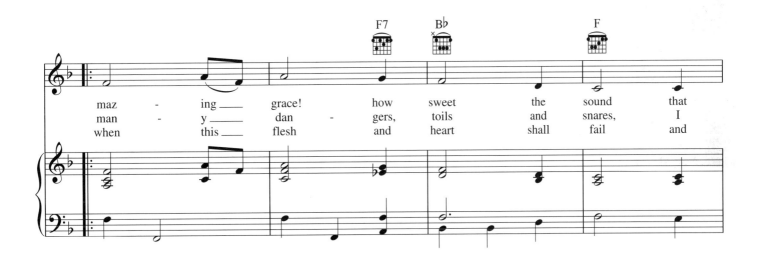

lost,   but   now ____ am ____ found,   was   blind,   but ____
brought   me   safe ____ thus ____ far,   and   grace   will ____
sess   with - in ____ the ____ veil   a   life   of ____

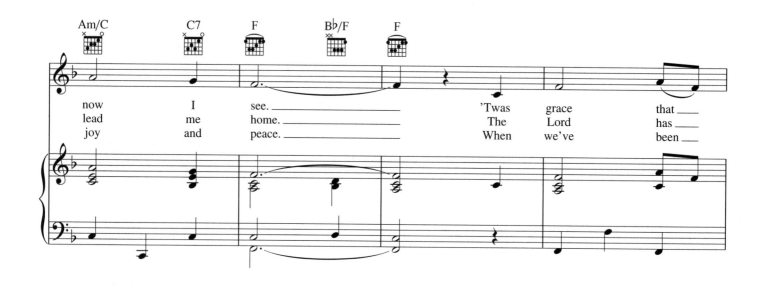

now   I   see. ____ 'Twas   grace   that ____
lead   me   home. ____ The   Lord   has ____
joy   and   peace. ____ When   we've   been ____

taught   my   heart   to   fear,   and   grace   my ____
prom - ised   good   to   me,   His   word   my ____
there   ten   thou - sand   years,   bright   shin - ing ____

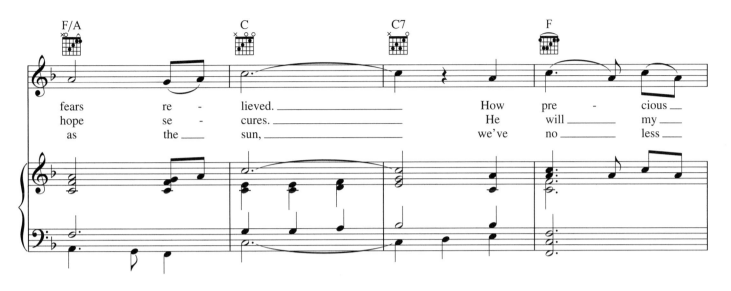

fears re - lieved. How pre - cious
hope se - cures. He will my
as the sun, we've no less

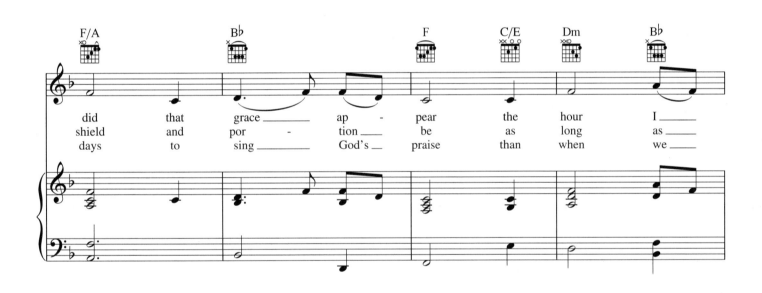

did that grace ap - pear the hour I
shield and por - tion be as long as
days to sing God's praise than when we

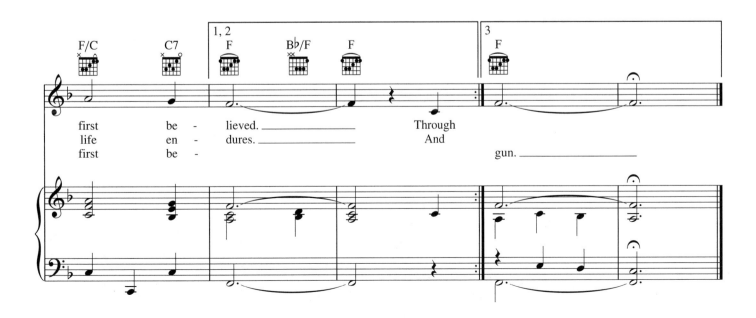

first be - lieved. Through
life en - dures. And
first be - gun.

Abide with Me

Words by Henry F. Lyte
Music by William H. Monk

All Creatures of Our God and King

Words by Francis of Assisi
Translated by William Henry Draper
Music from *Geistliche Kirchengesang*

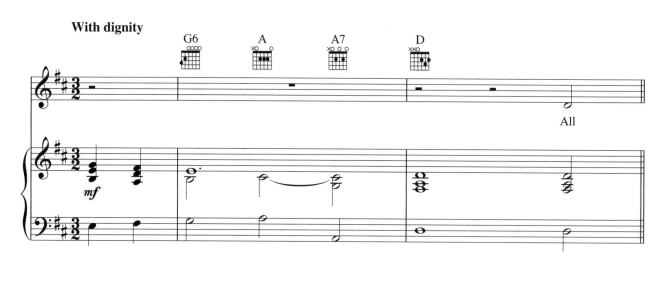

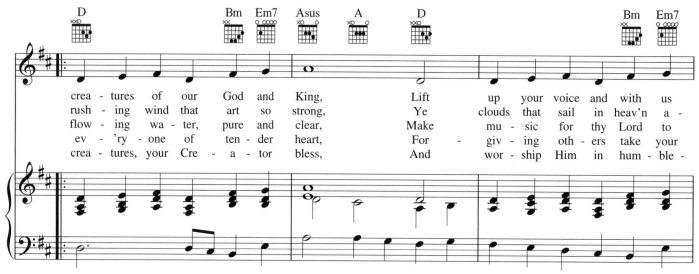

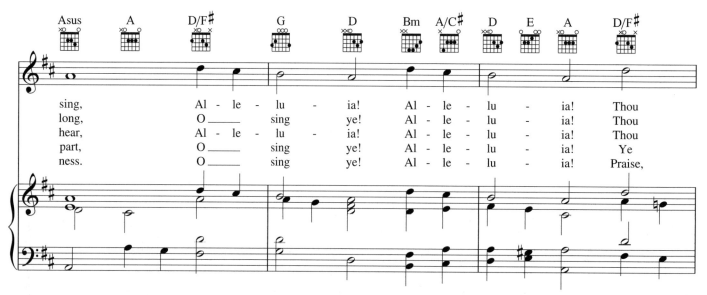

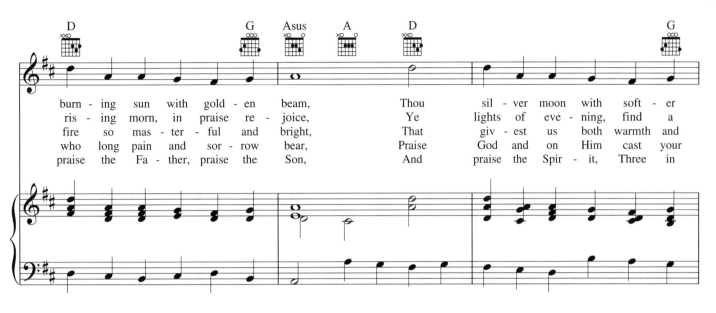

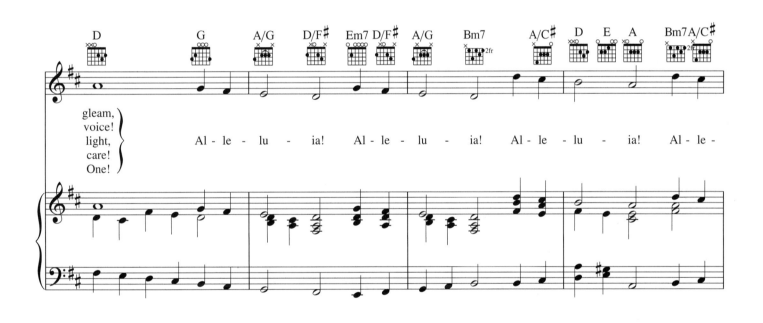

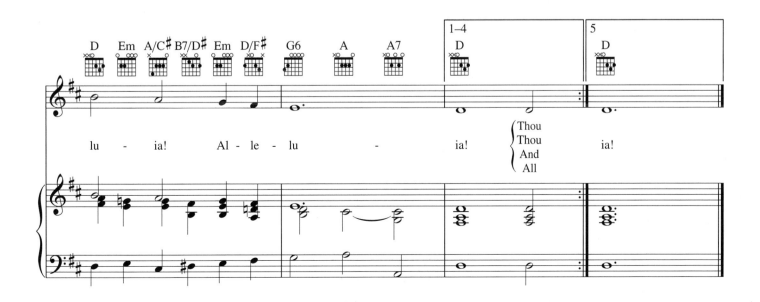

All My Trials

African-American Spiritual

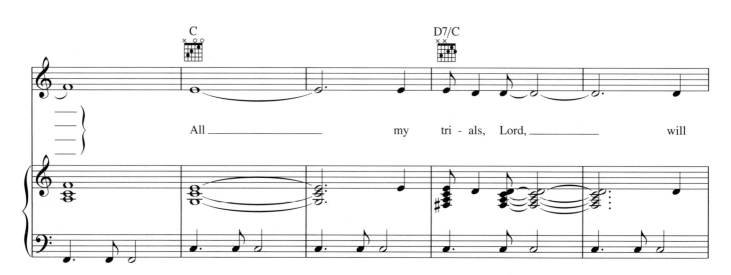

America, the Beautiful

Words by Katherine Lee Bates
Music by Samuel A. Ward

Moderately

1. O beau - ti - ful for spa - cious skies, for am - ber waves of
2. beau - ti - ful for pil - grim feet, whose stern, im - pas - sioned
3.,4. *(See additional verses)*

grain, for pur - ple moun - tain maj - es - ties a - bove the fruit - ed
stress, a thor - ough - fare for free - dom beat a - cross the wil - der -

plain! A - mer - i - ca! A - mer - i - ca! God shed His grace on
ness! A - mer - i - ca! A - mer - i - ca! God mend thine ev - ery

Additional Verses

3. O beautiful for heroes proved
   In liberating strife,
   Who more than self their country loved
   And mercy more than life!
   America! America!
   May God thy gold refine
   'Til all success be nobleness
   And every gain divine.

4. O beautiful for patriot dream
   That sees beyond the years;
   Thine alabaster cities gleam
   Undimmed by human tears.
   America! America!
   God shed His grace on thee,
   And crown thy good with brotherhood,
   From sea to shining sea.

Battle Hymn of the Republic

Words by Julia Ward Howe
Music by William Steffe

1. Mine eyes have seen the glo-ry of the com-ing of the Lord. He is
2. seen him in the watch-fires of the hun-dred cir-cling camps. They have
3.-5. *(See additional verses)*

tram-pling out the vin-tage where the grapes of wrath are stored. He hath
build-ed Him an al-tar in the eve-ning dews and damps. I have

loos'd the fate-ful light-ning of His ter-ri-ble swift sword. His
read His right-eous sen-tence by the dim and flar-ing lamps. His

Additional Verses

3. I have read a fiery gospel writ in burnished rows of steel.
   As ye deal with my contempters, so with you my grace shall deal.
   Let the hero born of woman crush the serpent with his heel,
   Since God is marching on.

4. He has sounded forth the trumpet that shall never call retreat.
   He is sifting out the hearts of men before His judgement seat.
   O be swift, my soul, to answer Him, be jubilant, my feet.
   Our God is marching on.

5. In the beauty of the lilies, Christ was born across the sea
   With a glory in His bosom that transfigures you and me.
   As He died to make men holy, let us die to make men free,
   While God is marching on.

Beautiful Isle of Somewhere

Words by Jessie B. Pounds
Music by John S. Fearis

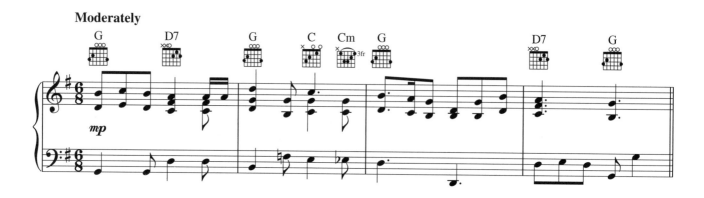

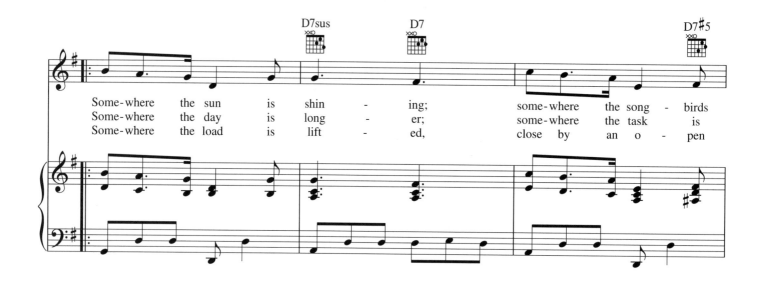

Some-where the sun is shin - ing; some-where the song - birds
Some-where the day is long - er; some-where the task is
Some-where the load is lift - ed, close by an o - pen

dwell. _____ Hush then thy sad re - pin - ing.
done. _____ Some-where the heart is strong - er;
gate. _____ Some-where the clouds are rift - ed,

Beautiful Savior

Words from *Munsterisch Gesangbuch*
Translated by Joseph A. Seiss
Music adapted from Silesian Folk Tune

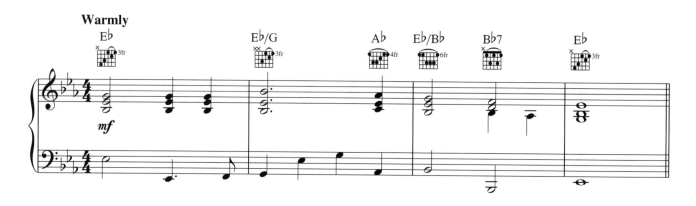

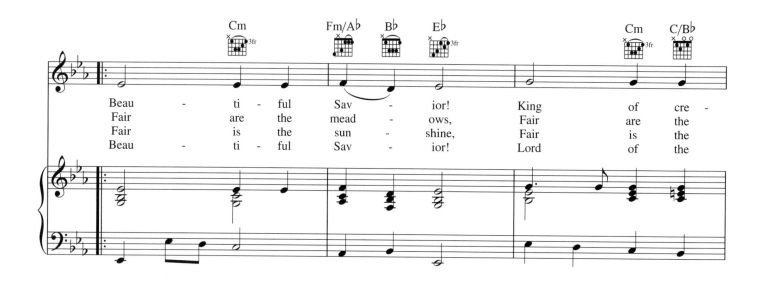

Beau - ti - ful Sav - ior! King of cre -
Fair are the mead - ows, Fair are the
Fair is the sun - shine, Fair is the
Beau - ti - ful Sav - ior! Lord of the

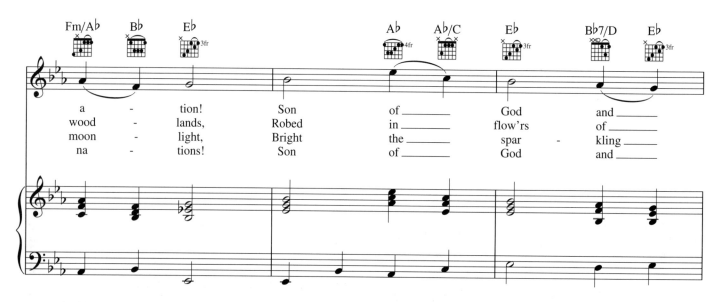

a - tion! Son of _____ God and _____
wood - lands, Robed in _____ flow'rs of _____
moon - light, Bright the _____ spar - kling _____
na - tions! Son of _____ God and _____

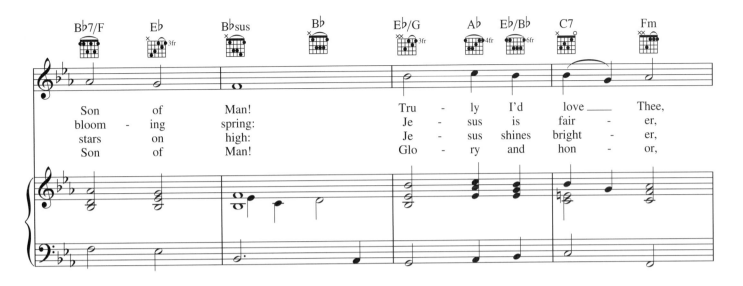

Son   of   Man!   Tru - ly   I'd   love ____ Thee,
bloom - ing   spring: Je - sus   is   fair - er,
stars   on   high: Je - sus shines bright - er,
Son   of   Man!   Glo - ry   and   hon - or,

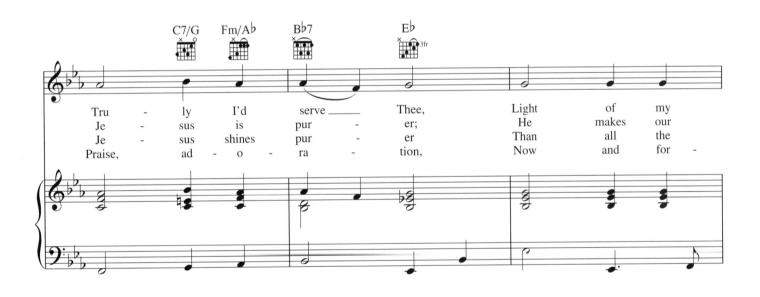

Tru - ly   I'd   serve ____ Thee,   Light   of   my
Je - sus   is   pur - er;   He   makes   our
Je - sus shines   pur - er   Than   all   the
Praise, ad - o - ra - tion,   Now   and   for -

soul,   my   joy,   my   crown.
sor -   r'wing   spir -   it   sing.
an -   gels   in   the   sky.
ev -   er -   more   be   Thine!

Bringing in the Sheaves

Words by Knowles Shaw
Music by George A. Minor

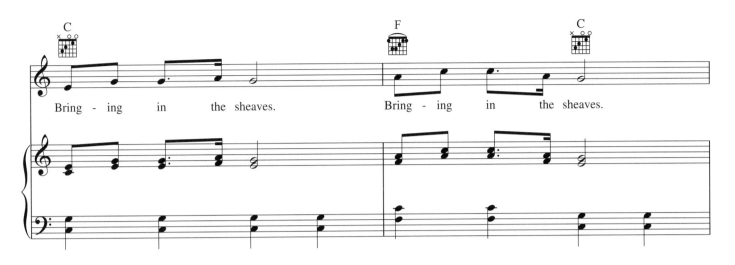

Bring - ing in the sheaves. Bring - ing in the sheaves.

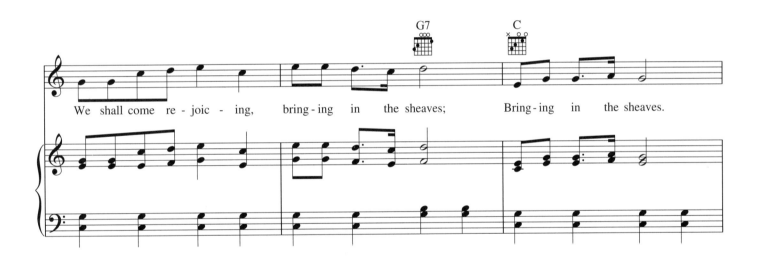

We shall come re - joic - ing, bring-ing in the sheaves; Bring-ing in the sheaves.

Bring-ing in the sheaves. We shall come re - joic - ing, Bring-ing in the sheaves.

A Child of the King

Words by Harriet E. Buell
Music by John B. Sumner

Moderately, with a lilt

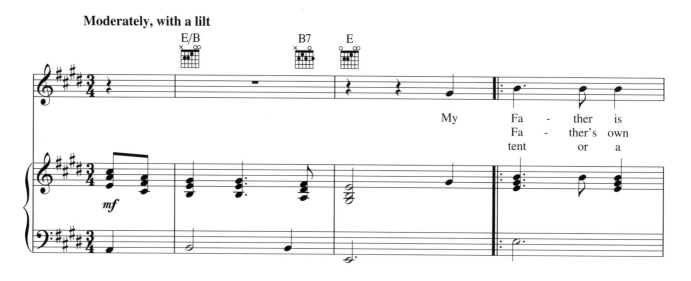

My   Fa - ther   is
Fa - ther's   own
tent   or   a

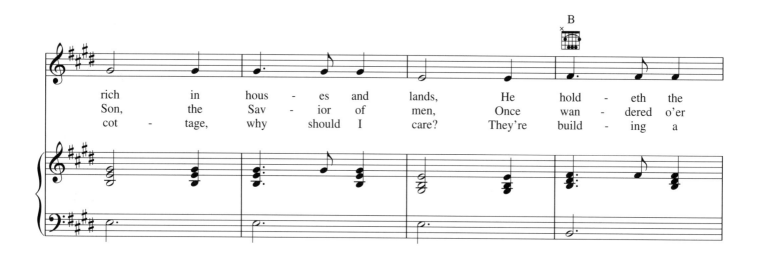

rich   in   hous - es   and   lands,   He   hold - eth   the
Son,   the   Sav - ior   of   men,   Once   wan - dered   o'er
cot - tage,   why   should   I   care?   They're   build - ing   a

wealth   of   the   world   in   His   hands!   Of   ru - bies   and
earth   as   the   poor - est   of   them;   But   now   He   is
pal - ace   for   me   o - ver   there!   Though   here   I'm   a

Christ the Lord Is Risen Today

Words by Charles Wesley
Music adapted from *Lyra Davidica*

Church in the Wildwood

Words and Music by Dr. William S. Pitts

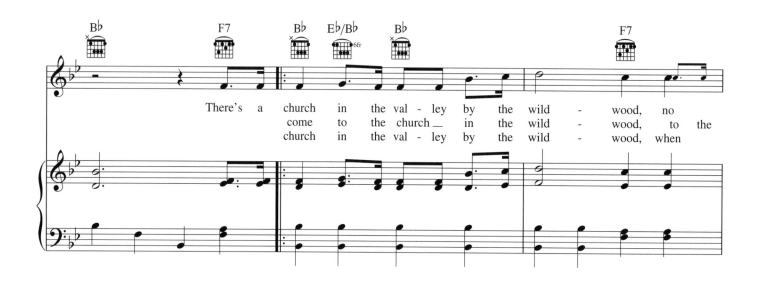

There's a church in the val - ley by the wild - wood, no
come to the church __ in the wild - wood, to the
church in the val - ley by the wild - wood, when

love - li - er spot in the dale.
trees where the wild - flow - ers bloom,
day fades a - way in - to night,

No __ place is so dear so my
where the part - ing __ hymn will be
I would fain from this spot of my

Close to Thee

Words by Fanny J. Crosby
Music by Silas J. Vail

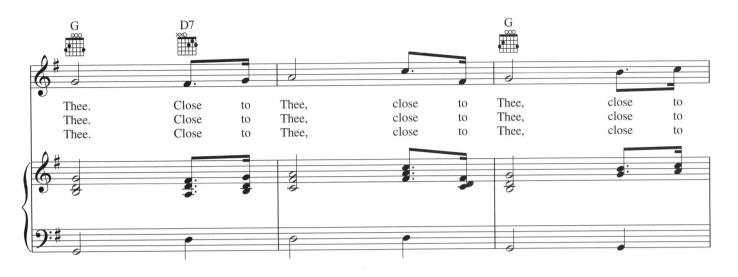

Thee.   Close   to   Thee,   close   to   Thee,   close   to
Thee.   Close   to   Thee,   close   to   Thee,   close   to
Thee.   Close   to   Thee,   close   to   Thee,   close   to

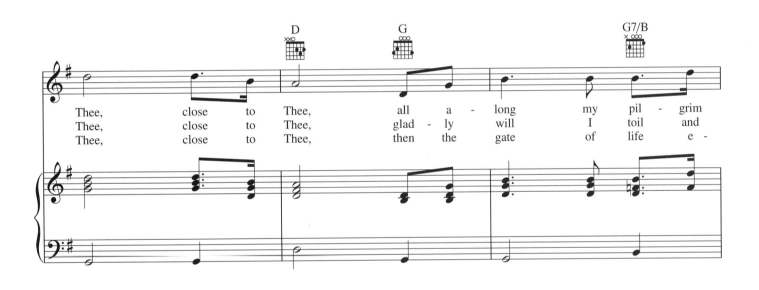

Thee,   close   to   Thee,   all   a - long   my   pil - grim
Thee,   close   to   Thee,   glad - ly   will   I   toil   and
Thee,   close   to   Thee,   then   the   gate   of   life   e -

jour - ney,   Sav - ior   let   me   walk   with   Thee.   Not   for
suf - fer,   on - ly   let   me   walk   with   Thee.   Lead   me
ter - nal   may   I   en - ter,   Lord,   with   Thee.

Come, Thou Almighty King

Traditional
Music by Felice de Giardini

Down by the Riverside

African-American Spiritual

Deep River

African-American Spiritual
Based on Joshua 3

Down at the Cross (Glory to His Name)

Words by Elisha A. Hoffman
Music by John H. Stockton

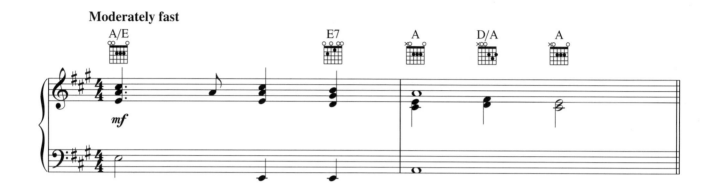

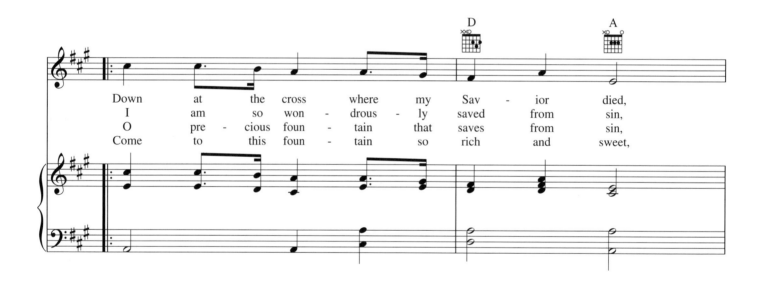

Down at the cross where my Sav - ior died,
I am so won - drous - ly saved from sin,
O pre - cious foun - tain that saves from sin,
Come to this foun - tain so rich and sweet,

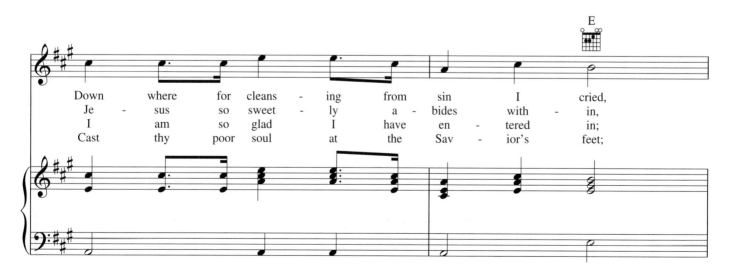

Down where for cleans - ing from sin I cried,
Je - sus so sweet - ly a - bides with - in,
I am so glad I have en - tered in;
Cast thy poor soul at the Sav - ior's feet;

Eternal Father, Strong to Save

Words by William Whiting
Music by John Bacchus Dykes

Additional Verses

2. O Savior, whose almighty word
   The winds and waves submissive heard,
   Who walkedst on the foaming deep
   and calm amid its rage didst sleep:
   O hear us when we cry to Thee
   For those in peril on the sea.

3. O sacred Spirit, who didst brood
   Upon the chaos dark and rude,
   Who bad'st its angry tumult cease.
   And gavest light and life and peace:
   O hear us when we cry to Thee
   For those in peril on the sea.

4. O Trinity of love and power,
   Our brethren shield in danger's hour;
   From rock and tempest, fire and foe,
   Protect them wheresoe'er they go;
   And ever let there rise to Thee
   Glad hymns of praise from land and sea. Amen.

Fairest Lord Jesus

Words from *Münster Gesangbuch*
Verse 4 by Joseph A. Seiss
Music from *Schlesische Volkslieder*
Arranged by Richard Storrs Willis

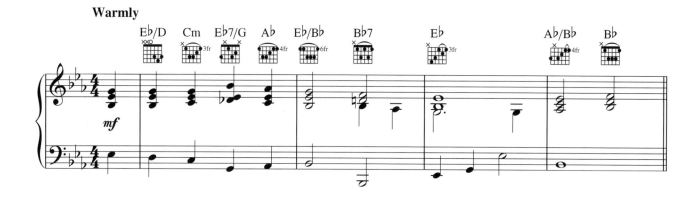

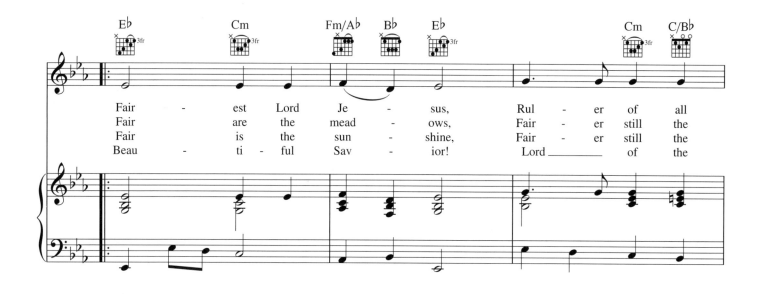

Fair - est Lord Je - sus, Rul - er of all
Fair are the mead - ows, Fair - er still the
Fair is the sun - shine, Fair - er still the
Beau - ti - ful Sav - ior! Lord _____ of the

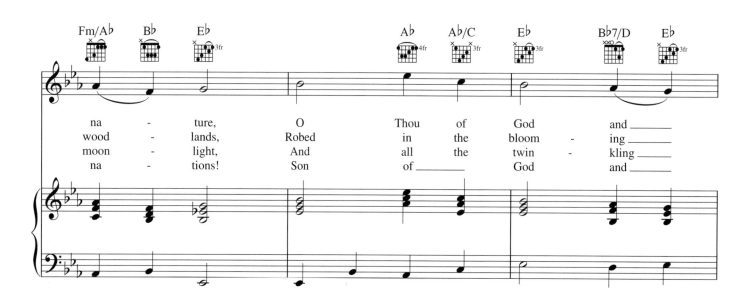

na - ture, O Thou of God and _____
wood - lands, Robed in the bloom - ing _____
moon - light, And all the twin - kling _____
na - tions! Son of _____ God and _____

Faith of Our Fathers

Words by Frederick William Faber
Music by Henri F. Hemy and James G. Walton

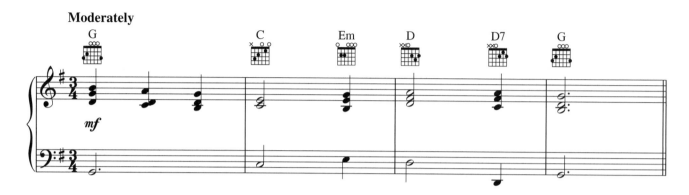

Faith of our fa - thers, liv - ing still
Faith of our fa - thers, we _____ will strive
Faith of our fa - thers, we _____ will love

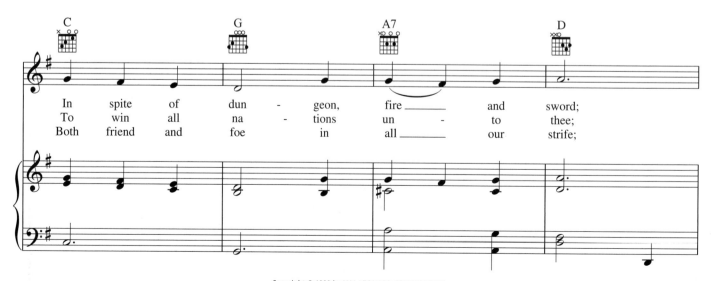

In spite of dun - geon, fire _____ and sword;
To win all na - tions un - to thee;
Both friend and foe in all _____ our strife;

Give Me That Old Time Religion

Traditional

Give me that old time re - li - gion, give me that old time re -

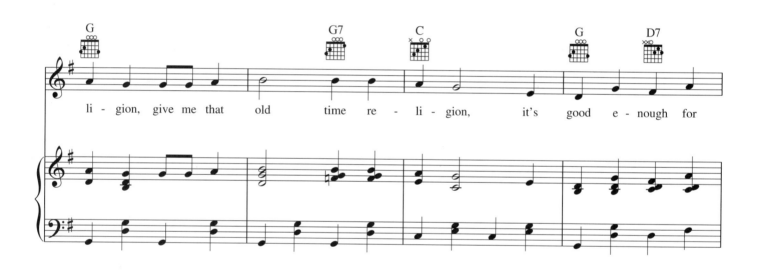

li - gion, give me that old time re - li - gion, it's good e - nough for

me. It was good for the He - brew chil - dren, It was
It will do when the world's on fi - re, It will

God Be with You Till We Meet Again

Words by Jeremiah E. Rankin
Music by William G. Tomer

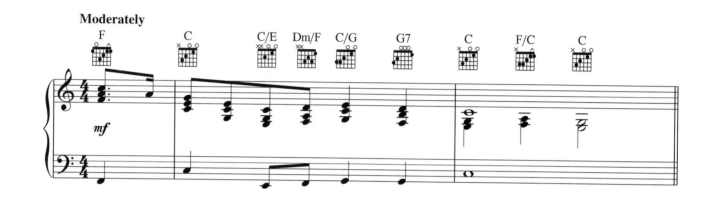

God be with you till we meet a - gain.

By His coun - sels guide, up -
'Neath His wings pro - tect - ing
When life's per - ils thick con -
Keep love's ban - ner float - ing

hold you, with His sheep se - cure - ly fold you.
hide you, dai - ly man - na still pro - vide you.
found you, put His arms un - fail - ing 'round you.
o'er you, smite death's threat - 'ning wave be - fore you.

God of Our Fathers

Words by Daniel Crane Roberts
Music by George William Warren

He's Got the Whole World in His Hands

Traditional Spiritual

He Leadeth Me

Words by Joseph H. Gilmore
Music by William B. Bradbury

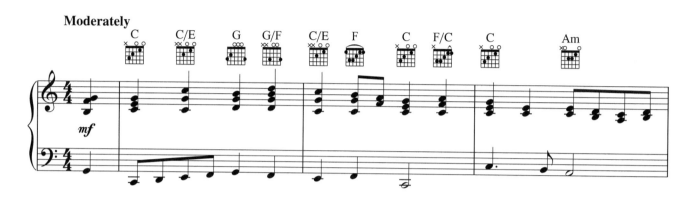

He lead - eth me! O bless - ed thought! O
times 'mid scenes of deep - est gloom, Some -
I would clasp Thy hand in mine, Nor
when my task on earth is done, When

words with heav'n - ly ___ com - fort fraught! What - e'er I do, where -
times where E - den's ___ bow - ers bloom, By wa - ters still, o'er
ev - er mur - mur ___ nor re - pine; Con - tent what - ev - er
by Thy grace the ___ vic - t'ry's won, E'en death's cold wave I

Holy, Holy, Holy

Text by Reginald Heber
Music by John B. Dykes

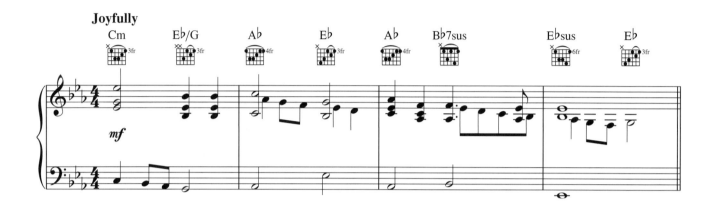

Ho - ly, ho - ly, ho - ly! Lord God Al -
Ho - ly, ho - ly, ho - ly! All the saints a -

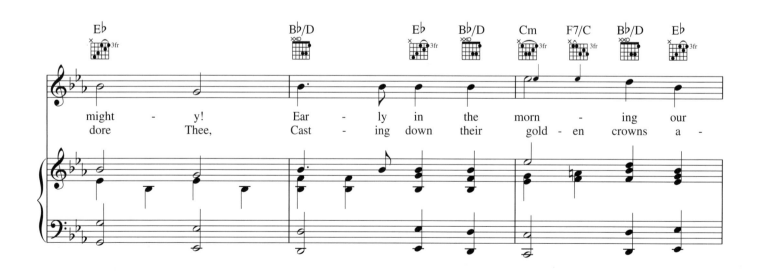

might - y! Ear - ly in the morn - ing our
dore Thee, Cast - ing down their gold - en crowns a -

In the Garden

Words and Music by C. Austin Miles

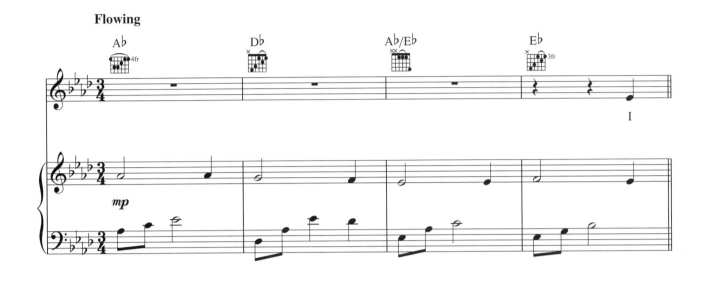

Flowing

I

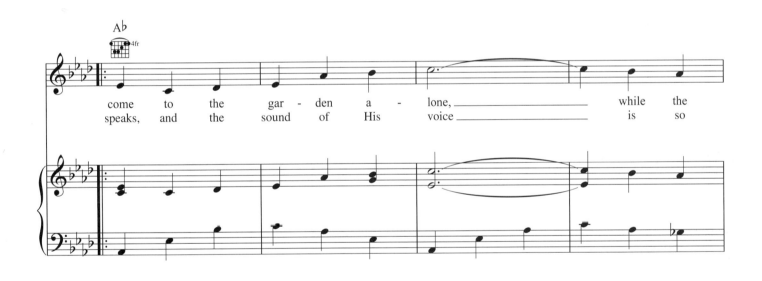

come to the gar - den a - lone, _____ while the
speaks, and the sound of His voice _____ is so

dew is still on the ros - es; and the
sweet the birds hush their sing - ing; and the

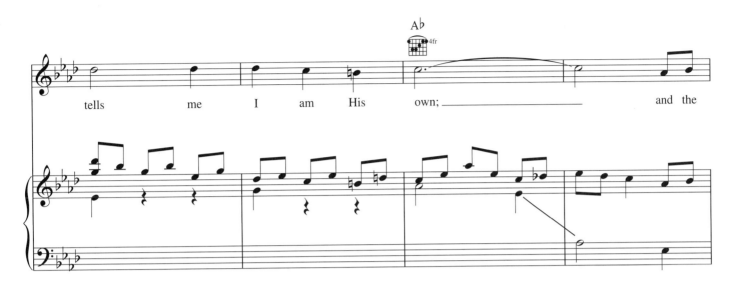

tells me I am His own; _____ and the

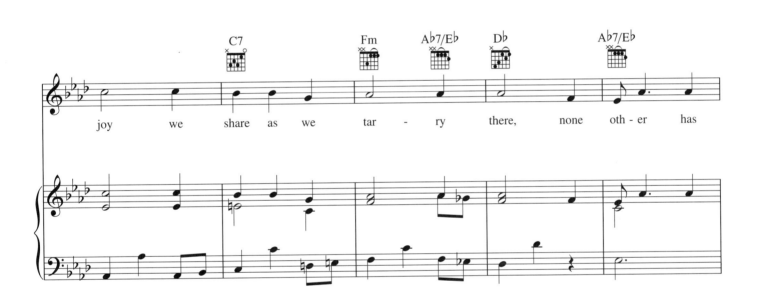

joy we share as we tar - ry there, none oth - er has

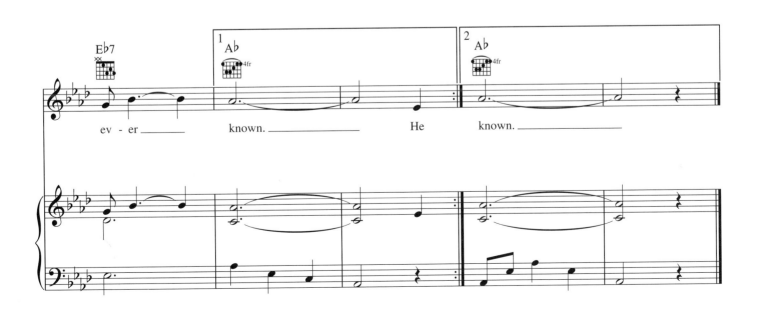

ev - er _____ known. _____ He known. _____

I Have Decided to Follow Jesus

Folk Melody from India
Arranged by Auila Read

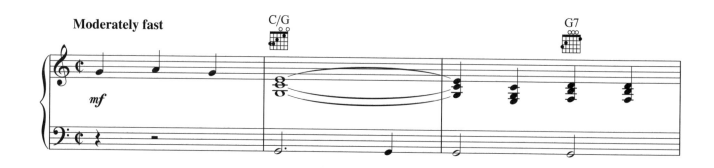

I have de - cid - ed _____ to fol - low
hind me. _____ the cross be -
with me, _____ still I will
cide now _____ to fol - low

Je - sus,   I have de - cid - ed _____
fore me,   the world be - hind me, _____
fol - low,   Though none go with me, _____
Je - sus?   Will you de - cide now _____

I Know That My Redeemer Lives

Words by Samuel Medley
Music by John Hatton

It Is Well with My Soul

Words by Horatio G. Spafford
Music by Philip P. Bliss

Peacefully

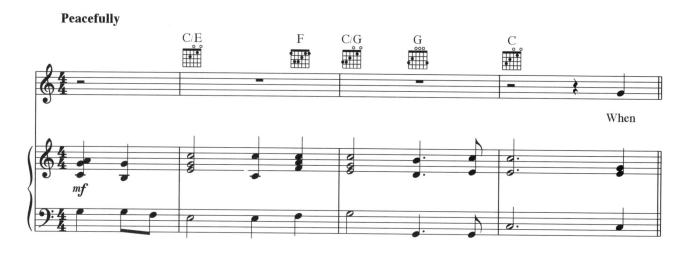

When

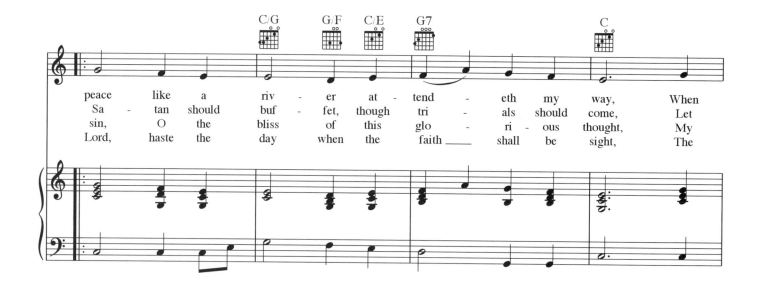

peace	like	a	riv - er	at - tend - eth	my	way,	When
Sa - tan	should	buf - fet,	though	tri - als	should	come,	Let
sin,	O the	bliss	of this	glo - ri - ous	thought,	My
Lord,	haste the	day	when the	faith ___ shall	be	sight,	The

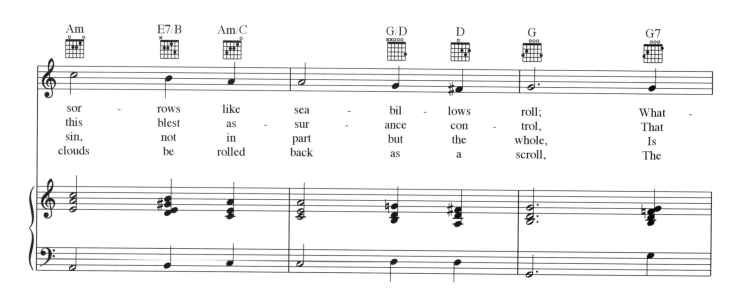

sor - rows	like	sea - bil - lows	roll;	What -
this blest	as - sur - ance	con - trol,	That
sin,	not in	part	but the	whole,	Is
clouds	be	rolled	back	as	a	scroll,	The

Jesus, Keep Me Near the Cross

Words by Fanny J. Crosby
Music by William H. Doane

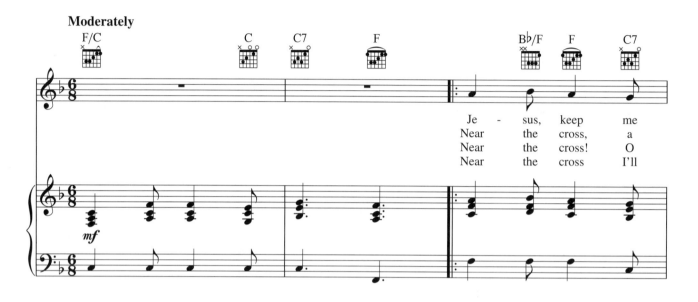

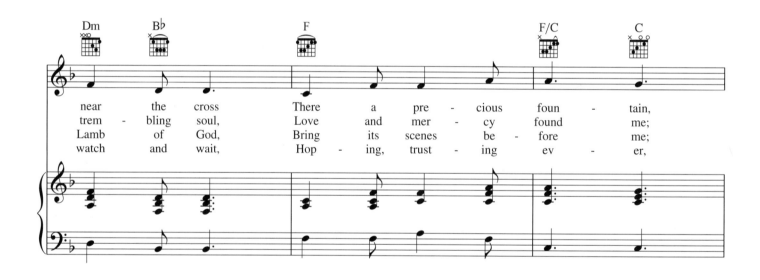

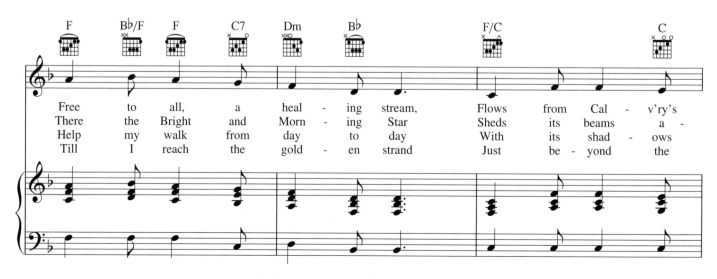

moun - tain.
round me.
o'er me.
riv - er.

In the cross, in the cross

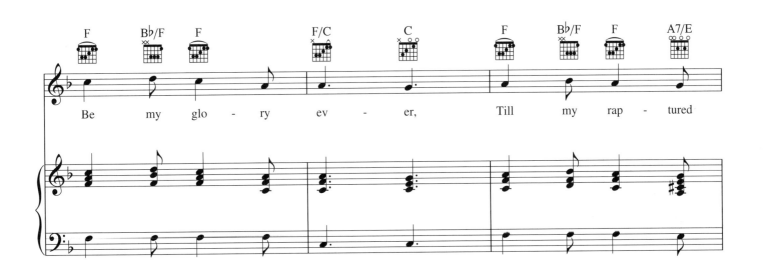

Be my glo - ry ev - er, Till my rap - tured

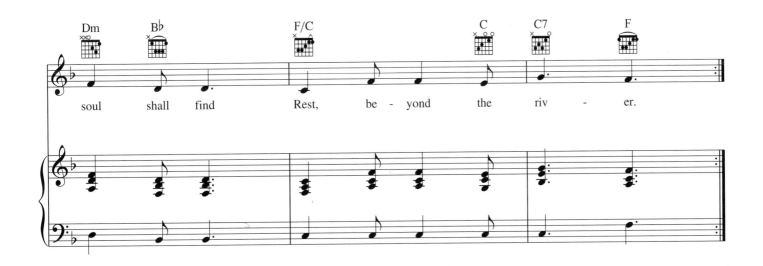

soul shall find Rest, be - yond the riv - er.

Jesus, Thou Joy of Loving Hearts

Words attributed to Bernard of Clairvaux
Translated by Ray Palmer
Music by Henry Baker

Just a Closer Walk with Thee

Traditional
Arranged by Kenneth Morris

Performance Notes

Abide with Me (page 10)

The man who wrote this hymn about death and dying once remarked, "It is better to wear out than rust." Well, Henry Lyte definitely lived up to his word. He was a poet, musician, and minister in the Church of England during the first half of the 19th century. Although he suffered from asthma and tuberculosis for most of his adult life he worked tirelessly. In fact, Lyte almost crawled to the pulpit to deliver his final message before dying of tuberculosis in 1847. Despite the depressing nature of Henry Lyte's lot in life and death, the hymn is widely used for weddings, including the matrimonial ceremony of King George VI and the royal wedding of his daughter, Queen Elizabeth II. "Abide with Me" was also a favorite of two prominent world figures, Mahatma Gandhi and Mother Teresa.

This hymn text is in the form of a prayer. It should be played quietly and with reverence. Connect the notes in a smooth legato style. A *ritard,* which is a slowing of the tempo, into the first and second ending is appropriate. The tempo should be as indicated, moderately slow. Don't be in a hurry with this reflective text. The key of E♭ isn't the easiest to play, so be careful with all the flats in the key signature and watch out for an occasional accidental, which changes that note for the entire bar. You could make a more satisfying ending by repeating the last line, "In life, in death, O Lord, abide with me."

All Creatures of Our God and King (page 12)

This hymn is found in almost every Christian hymnal regardless of denomination. It is also one of the religion's oldest and most recognizable tunes. Written around 1225 by Saint Francis of Assisi, this well-known tune has survived for nearly 800 years. Saint Francis did not found PETA (People for the Ethical Treatment of Animals) or Greenpeace, but he surely serves as the oldest inspiration for these organizations. Saint Francis of Assisi is the patron saint of the animals and the environment in the Roman Catholic Church. In 1223, Saint Francis created the first nativity scene including live persons and animals. This medieval Franciscan monk wrote over 60 hymns, but "All Creatures of Our God and King" is the only one that has survived the centuries. The version we sing today was translated into English and paraphrased by William Draper at the turn of the 20th century.

This is one of the oldest tunes in active use in Christian hymnody. With half note beats it is important to be deliberate in tempo. This is what musicians often call a *sturdy* melody. Play it with a firm touch, being careful to bring out the quarter notes that are each a half beat, while sustaining the half notes. The moving notes in the left hand part are important. The bass part really carries the tune. The *Alleluias* at the end should be emphasized to close out this sacred classic.

All My Trials (page 14)

What do Joan Baez, Elvis Presley, Paul McCartney, Harry Belafonte, Pete Seeger, Ray Stevens, and Peter, Paul & Mary have in common? They have all sung and recorded versions of this 19th century Bahamian ballad. This simple folk tune originated in the 1800s and was based on Revelation 21:4, "He will wipe every tear from their eyes. There will be no more death or mourning or crying or pain, for the old order of things has passed away." In the 1950s and 1960s, "All My Trials" became a staple of the folk music circuit and was used to reference social protest movements such as Civil Rights and the Vietnam War. Elvis Presley used the hymn in the 1970s as part of "An American Trilogy," a medley that included "All My Trials," "Dixie," and "Battle Hymn of the Republic." Most recently, Paul McCartney released a live version of the song in the 1990s, which even made the Top 40 list in the United Kingdom. The message and appeal of this hymn remain timeless.

Because this folk song is based on an African-American spiritual, it should be played with a relaxed feel. Try to emulate the sound of a strumming guitar with the right hand while the left hand carries the bass line. Feel free to take the left hand bass note down an octave occasionally to give it a little more depth and add to the interest. Also, on the long sustained chords in the right hand you can add some quarter notes to keep the song in tempo. Resist the tendency you may have to rush through the song. Even though the ending says to repeat and fade, just find a good place to sustain a C major chord and call it quits.

Amazing Grace (page 7)

The Trans-Atlantic slave trade killed an estimated two million Africans and served as one of the darkest chapters in the history of western civilization. Ironically, the hymn "Amazing Grace" emerged from an unlikely source, the captain of a slave ship. On a long journey from Brazil in the mid-1700s, John Newton and his crew met a powerful storm that threatened to sink their ship. On that same journey Newton had taken interest in a book that had been given to him, Thomas à Kempis' *The Imitation of Christ*. Newton had a conversion experience on that trip that led him to trade in his sea legs for the pulpit. He became a minister in the Anglican Church and began his pastorate in the village of Olney near Cambridge, England. The hymn was written in near obscurity in an attic room where Newton wrote his sermons and weekly hymns. It was first heard in 1773 and became part of the *Olney Hymns* hymnal (1779), a collection of 349 hymns written by John Newton and William Cowper. As famous as the hymn is today, the music we associate with "Amazing Grace" was not added until 1835, over 60 years after its inception. Interestingly, John Newton passed away in 1807, just as Great Britain passed a resolution to abolish slavery.

"Amazing Grace" is probably the best-known sacred song in western culture. It has been performed in many different genres and styles, from a solo harmonica to full orchestra and chorus. There are many different approaches to this simple yet profound song. The first choice is whether to play the eighth notes in an even style, called *straight eighths,* or with a triplet feel, called *swing eighths.* Either will work just fine. The bass line is important so bring it out as you play. Added quarter notes in the right hand will keep the rhythm going. The song has several other verses not included here that you might want to include. You'll easily find them in hymnbooks and songbooks (or online). The accompaniment given here will work perfectly with all the verses.

America, the Beautiful (page 16)

"America, the Beautiful" remains a melodic, simple hymn containing lyrics so descriptive that most picture "amber waves of grain" blowing in the wind under "spacious skies" as they sing. In fact, many have suggested that this patriotic tune be made the national anthem over the war-oriented, vocally challenging "Star Spangled Banner." Katherine Lee Bates, Chair of the English Department at Wellesley College, penned the unforgettable words of "America, the Beautiful." Although she wrote several academic books, Bates' biggest legacy remains the poem that became the nation's second most popular patriotic hymn. She wrote it after visiting Pike's Peak in Colorado, and one can follow her journey to the Rocky Mountains using her lyrics as a map and guide through America's landscape. The poem was published in 1904, but Bates never intended for it to be sung. Ultimately, the lyrics were matched with a previously written tune entitled "O Mother Dear, Jerusalem" (1882) by Samuel Augustus Ward. Today, Ray Charles' rendition of "America, the Beautiful" remains the most popular recording of the song.

Start off this hymn with a more reserved and quiet manner and build up to the climactic phrase at the bottom of the page, "America! America! God shed His grace on thee." Patriotic hymns should generally be performed in a stately style with sustained, even quarter notes. A big slowdown or *ritard* at the end will bring a fitting close to this poetic hymn. This is a popular tune for patriotic holidays so it would be a good one to have ready to play and sing.

Battle Hymn of the Republic (page 18)

When Julia Ward Howe visited the Union Army encampment on the Potomac River, she was inspired when she heard the men singing "John Brown's Body." John Brown was an eccentric and controversial abolitionist who had led several anti-slavery rallies and raids following the Kansas-Nebraska Act in the 1850s. After his capture and hanging, John Brown was hailed as a martyr in the North and a madman in the South. He was a little bit of both. When Howe first heard the song she loved the tune, but decided it needed better words. She penned the famous lyrics almost immediately and remarked, "I scrawled the verses almost without looking at the paper." The hymn was published in the *Atlantic Monthly* in 1862. When the hymn was performed at a rally attended by Abraham Lincoln, he reportedly cried out, "Sing it again" with tears in his eyes. It remains one of America's most beloved patriotic tunes.

Some pieces of music call for precise rhythmic performance, and this is one of them. Be careful with the dotted eighths and sixteenth rhythms that are so prevalent in this song so that they don't come out with a triplet feel. Because this song is performed in a march-like style, keep the left hand fairly short and articulated. Don't let the open fifths run together. Accent the measures with four quarter notes to help highlight the text "His truth is marching on." The natural or *agogic* beats on one and three will naturally be a little heavier on this song. That's the way marches are.

Beautiful Isle of Somewhere (page 20)

This hymn speaks of an island but was written in the Midwest far from any ocean. Jessie Pounds lived in Ohio and moved to Indiana after marrying the Reverend John Pounds in 1896. At the early age of 15, Pounds began submitting poems, short stories, and articles to local newspapers and religious publishing houses. Although most of her submissions were rejected, one editor suggested that she use her texts to write songs. She took his suggestion to heart, and by the end of her lifetime, Pounds had written over 400 gospel songs. Still, "Beautiful Isle of Somewhere," written in 1897, remains her most famous composition. For over 30 years, Pounds collaborated with James Fillmore, one of the siblings who founded the Fillmore Brothers Music House in Cincinnati, Ohio. This hymn was sung at the funeral of William McKinley following his 1901 assassination. It was President McKinley's favorite song.

There's an Italian song form called a *siciliana* that is reminiscent of this song. The *siciliana* gets it name from the island of Sicily and the gentle rocking motion of the gondolas there. *Sicilianas* are always in 6/8 with flowing broken chords. That's exactly the style for this tune. Keep that even flow to the rhythm. Gondolas would be a natural mode of transportation to the "Beautiful Isle of Somewhere."

Beautiful Savior (page 22)

This hymn was written by German Jesuits and first entitled "Schönster Herr Jesu" in the 17th century. It is widely known as the "Crusader's Hymn." Joseph Seiss, a Lutheran pastor in the United States, translated it into English in 1873. The origins of the lyrics remain a mystery, but many argue that the words date back to the 12th century as Crusaders set out for the Holy Land. Others believe that the hymn was sung by followers of John Hus, an anti-Reformation leader in the early 1600s, who lived in Silesia (modern-day Poland). The music was arranged by Richard Storrs Willis who also composed the Christmas carol "It Came Upon the Midnight Clear."

Smooth is the concept best applied to this hymn tune. Sustain the melody with notes in full value. The accompaniment is very simple so some added quarter note chords or arpeggiated notes will add interest to the performance. *Arpeggios* are chords that are broken up, usually bottom to top, instead of all the notes being played at once. With four verses, some variation in the piano will keep all the music from sounding the same. This same tune will be found with the title "Fairest Lord Jesus" in many hymnals as well, with the same tune, text, and harmony.

Bringing in the Sheaves *(page 24)*

Long beards were fairly common in the mid-1800s, but Knowles Shaw's facial fabric would certainly earn honors in the World Beard and Moustache Championships. Shaw had a talent for facial hair, but then he excelled at just about everything. He was self-trained in carpentry, watch making, shoe making, sewing, piano, and violin. He was also fluent in Greek and Latin. One neighbor commented, "Knowles Shaw's head was like a tar-bucket, for everything that touched it stuck to it." His musical talents led him to write this hymn in addition to becoming a prolific preacher and orator in the 1860s and 1870s. Shaw lived a dramatic life full of vigor and intensity, and he died under dramatic circumstances as well. While traveling to McKinney, Texas, the train derailed, flipped three times, and fell 40 feet before landing in a pool of water. Shaw was killed in the crash but not before helping a fellow passenger to safety.

This hymn is based on the agrarian concept of bringing in the crops and is a fun tune with a feel similar to a march. Accent the notes on beats one and three and keep the dotted eighth and sixteenth rhythms crisp. The song doesn't have an introduction, so consider playing the last two bars as an intro to set the tempo and give the singers the key for this song. This setting is pitched on the high side so play with firmness and confidence to help the singers get those high notes! Repeating the last two bars as an extended ending is also a good idea.

A Child of the King *(page 26)*

Harriet Beull wrote a poem walking home from church in Manlius, New York. She sent the poem to the *Northern Christian Advocate,* and it was published in 1877. In another part of the state, music teacher and preacher John Sumner read Beull's poem and realized that the lyrics were perfect for a hymn he was composing. Copyrights and patents worked a bit differently in the 19th century, and Sumner wrote the music and published the hymn as a complete work without Harriet Beull's permission or knowledge. Imagine her surprise when she heard her poem sung as a hymn during a regular Sunday night service in Manlius. Fortunately for Sumner and Beull, neither sought to challenge the intellectual property rights and the hymn became immensely popular.

Many piano players would rather play songs in flats than sharps and learn a common trick of playing pieces like this one in A major in A♭ major instead. The notes are all the same; just change the key signature. When you come across a natural sign as an accidental, just play it as a flat. Whether you play this song in sharps or flats, keep it in a simple 3/4 with even eighths. You can easily substitute some broken chords, or simple arpeggios, in place of some of the repeated quarter notes.

Christ the Lord Is Risen Today (page 28)

Many know that John Wesley is credited with founding the Methodist denomination within the Protestant church. His brother Charles was also instrumental, no pun intended, in the formation of Methodism. Charles Wesley wrote over 6,000 hymns including *Collection of Hymns for the Use of the People Called Methodists* published in 1779. However, this Easter favorite serves as Charles Wesley's largest contribution to the western world of hymnology. Charles did not compose the melody but loved the tune, regardless of a rhythmic mismatch. Thus, the lingering refrain of "Alleluia" was added to help the song's overall flow. Hundreds of Wesley's hymns were printed throughout Great Britain, but songs were commonly altered and reprinted without consent. As only the British can, John Wesley responded both harshly and politely, "I must beg two favours: either let [the hymns] stand just as they are . . . or add the true reading in the margin . . . that we may no longer be accountable either for the nonsense or for the doggerel of other men."

Sometimes seasonal songs like this are more difficult to play, mainly because they are used only once a year. This arrangement is on the heavy side with a lot of octaves in the left hand. If you have trouble reaching so many octaves in a row, just play a single note in either octave. Add the octaves on big *cadences* at the end on C major. A *cadence* is the last two chords of a musical phrase. Though it asks for the piece to be played *Joyfully*, don't let that allow the tempo to get too fast. This arrangement doesn't have an introduction. For a stately tune like this, the piano player may play the hymn all the way through as an introduction.

Church in the Wildwood (page 30)

The words and music of this hymn were written by Dr. William S. Pitts based not on a "Church in the Wildwood," but rather the vision of a church in rural Bradford, Iowa. To his amazement, a church was in fact erected in the exact spot that he had envisioned years earlier. In 1862, Pitts helped dedicate the "Little Brown Church" with this song. Pitts sold the rights to the song to pay his tuition for medical school and graduated in 1868. The church in Iowa fell into disrepair in the 1870s and closed in 1888. The song was also forgotten but resurrected in 1914 as the "Little Brown Church" was revived. The Weatherwax Quartet, a traveling singing group in the early 1900s, sang the song regularly as they canvassed the country. Today, the "Church in the Wildwood" remains a treasured song and the church itself is a frequented tourist site in Bradford.

Try to imagine yourself playing in a country church on an old piano that is a bit out of tune back in the 1930s. Be firm and rhythmic. Keep a crisp melody in the right hand and solid accented quarters in the left hand. This was, and is, a popular sing-along song recalling olden days. Be a little softer at the start of the chorus and build to the end. Many folks will recall a commonly used choral background part to the chorus. If they want to sing it, it will fit right into the melody.

Close to Thee (page 32)

In May of 1820, Fanny Crosby developed a severe cold and cough at six weeks of age. Her parents, John and Mercy, did not have a great deal of wealth and settled for a self-proclaimed "doctor" to see Fanny after failing to reach their physician. He turned out to be worse than a snake oil salesman, for he recommended mustard plasters to treat her cold and accompanying eye infection. Mustard plasters were commonly used to stimulate healing, but were only used inside a protective dressing and applied on the chest or back to adults and children over six years of age. This doctor placed the mustard plasters on her eyes, blistering and burning her eyes. The procedure blinded her for life. Crosby certainly rebounded with tenacity and faith, becoming perhaps the most prolific American lyricist within Protestantism. She wrote over

8,000 hymns in her life including "Jesus Is Tenderly Calling," "To God Be the Glory," and of course "Close to Thee." At the age of 95, Fanny Crosby passed away. Her epitaph echoes one of Crosby's most popular hymns and her personal favorite, "Blessed Assurance, Jesus is mine, Oh what a foretaste of glory divine."

"Close to Thee" is quiet and reflective, so the performance style should be smooth and even. Don't worry too much about the dotted eighth and sixteenth rhythms. You can cheat on them a little and make them sound more triplet-like. This song is pitched on the high side in G major, so be firm on the piano when the voice is in the upper range. Play some repeated quarter notes on the same notes written as half notes to keep the tempo from dragging.

Come, Thou Almighty King (page 34)

This war hymn is widely used as an opening call to worship. Some argue that Charles Wesley authored the lyrics, but many maintain the author is simply unknown. The hymn dates back to the mid-1700s and first appeared in George Whitefield's *Collection of Hymns for Social Worship*. By the 1770s, war seemed inevitable between Great Britain and the American colonies. During this time a new adaptation of the song emerged. The British version was entitled "God Save Our Gracious King" while pro-independence colonists sang, "Come, Thou Almighty King." It was like two versions of the same cheer at a high school football game. Both groups used the hymn to justify war and inspire patriotism, and the lyrics are intended to invoke the support of the Trinity. The first three verses appeal separately to the Father, Son, and Holy Spirit for strength and power in battle. The Italian composer Felice de Giardini wrote the music specifically used for the American version of this hymn.

Another sturdy melody is the *Italian Hymn* that is most often associated with "Come, Thou Almighty King." Even though it is in 3/4 time, it has a march-like feel to it. Some repeated quarter notes on the dotted half note chords will keep the energy level going. A slight *ritard,* or slowing of the tempo, on the last phrase of the last verse is appropriate. For an introduction, start three bars before the first ending to set the tempo and give the singers the key for the song.

Deep River (page 40)

There is a town in Ontario, Canada named Deep River, but this song is about a more metaphorical water flow. The hymn "Deep River" is an American slave spiritual that describes physical freedom as well as eternal emancipation in the afterlife. H.L. Mencken, author of *The American Language* and Scopes Trial reporter, argued that the unknown composer of "Deep River" also might have written "Swing Low, Sweet Chariot" and "Roll, Jordan, Roll." All of these spirituals deal with the heartache of enslavement and the promise of freedom, gained either in life or death. Crossing the "river" to reach the "campground" on the other side symbolized freedom both literally and figuratively. In a literal sense, crossing the Ohio River signaled escape from the slave state of Kentucky to the free state of Ohio. The Fisk Jubilee Singers, Fisk University's world-renowned African-American choir, often sang this hymn in the late 19th century, and it remains a part of their repertoire to the present day.

"Deep River" is more of a solo song that one person would sing rather than a hymn for group singing. The piano part is more "pianistic" and doesn't simply follow the melodic line. The melody is wide ranging, covering an octave and a sixth. That's wider than the range of the "Star Spangled Banner" by a step. Singers will need a firm touch on the line "that promised land," so be ready to lend support. This song has a *D.S. al Coda.* Play to the *D.S. al Coda* sign, and then go back to the 𝄋 at the beginning of measure three. The second time around you'll jump from the *coda* sign (⊕) to the *coda* at the end.

Down at the Cross (Glory to His Name) (page 42)

This hymn is a regular in Sunday morning church services, but is also often titled "Glory to His Name." Elisha Hoffman was a minister who served congregations in Ohio, Michigan, Illinois, and Pennsylvania. He edited over 50 songbooks and wrote the lyrics for over 2,000 gospel songs that also included: "I Must Tell Jesus," "Are You Washed in the Blood?" and "Leaning on the Everlasting Arms." John Hart Stockton, a well-known musician and minister in the Methodist Episcopal Church, composed the music for this piece. He also wrote the words and music for the popular hymns "Take Me as I Am" and "Only Trust Him." The hymn dates back to the 1870s and is always a congregational favorite with its simple melody and message.

This is a tune arranged in A major that may be played in A♭ major by changing the key signature mentally to four flats and playing the notes on the page "as is." It's a simple way that many piano players are able to play a song in flats rather than sharps. Depending on your early piano training and experience, sometimes flat keys are more comfortable. Don't let the accidentals throw you off. Natural signs in sharp keys become flats in the flat key, and the sharps in the sharp key will become naturals. Adding quarter notes or additional repeated bass notes to this march-style song keeps the rhythm moving along.

Down by the Riverside (page 35)

The Book of Isaiah, Chapter 2, inspired this song, which contains many pointed phrases directed toward the Civil War, northern/southern sectionalism, and racism. Isaiah, the Biblical figure, is paraphrased in the chorus, "I'm gonna lay down my sword and shield, Down by the riverside . . . And study war no more." Although the origins of this spiritual date back to the Civil War, the song serves as another example of the power of water as a symbol of freedom. The words speak of hope despite hardship and also suggest a personal transformation from violence toward peace. Several versions appeared between 1865 and the 1930s based mainly on regional and racial differences in dialect. The Fisk Jubilee Singers were the first to record the hymn in 1920, and it was published in a collection of tunes entitled *American Songbag* (1927). In the 1960s, "Down by the Riverside" was revived and used by many who protested the conflict in Vietnam. It remains an American Folk classic with its catchy chorus and positive message.

The Dixieland musical performance style is characterized by strong accents on beats one and three, so let the left hand be the tuba or string bass that drives the song. The right hand plays the chords like a banjo, so keep it strumming in a light moving style. No heavy-handedness, please. The song will be best performed in a slow two-beat per bar manner rather than four beats per bar. Singers will tend to slide around the notes in a bluesy fashion, but that's stylistically correct for an up-tempo and jazzy spiritual song like "Down by the Riverside."

Eternal Father, Strong to Save (page 44)

This song was featured heavily in the motion picture blockbuster *Titanic* in 1997. After reading the lyrics, one can easily see why this tune was selected by writer and director James Cameron. In the United States the song is also known as the "Navy Hymn." However, it began as a Royal Naval Hymn for Great Britain. William Whiting of Winchester, England penned the lyrics in 1860. Whiting wrote it as a poem for a former student who was departing for the United States. John B. Dykes put the words to music with his tune entitled "Melita." This title was also no accident as the archaic name Melita translates to Malta. Malta was the ancient seafaring island nation where the Apostle Paul was rescued after his shipwreck off the coast of Greece. The U.S. Navy Band played this hymn for the funerals of Franklin D. Roosevelt and John F. Kennedy, as both men had previously served in the Navy. The hymn and its history certainly invoke images of storm, shipwreck, and death by sea. Fortunately William Whiting's student, for whom the poem was written, journeyed across the Atlantic without incident and arrived safely in the United States.

As the *Navy Hymn,* the standing joke among musicians is that this song has a lot of "fluid" harmony. Actually, there is a lot of *chromaticism* (sharps and flats) in this tune, so be careful with all the accidentals. Although the *chromatics* make the tune more difficult to play, they also make the chords very interesting to the listener. Keep the eighth notes smooth, and connect the melody and chords in a legato style.

Fairest Lord Jesus *(page 46)*

This hymn is essentially the same as "Beautiful Savior." See the notes on "Beautiful Savior" for the history of the tune and text. There are two verses that are different, but they were written by the same author. The reason is unknown as to why some denominational hymnals use the title "Fairest Lord Jesus," and others use "Beautiful Savior" or "Crusader's Hymn." Either way it is a lovely marriage of text and tune.

You can perform this well-known traditional hymn a couple of different ways. Traditionally you would keep the chords nice and solid in a four beat per bar style. Another approach is to take the song in a two beat per bar tempo and add some flowing eighth notes in place of the half-note chords to make it a more lyrical presentation. Either style will work fine. The key of E♭ should be fairly comfortable for pianists.

Faith of Our Fathers *(page 48)*

It would seem from the title that this hymn is all about men; however, it was actually written in honor of a woman. Catherine of Alexandria lived in Egypt during the third and fourth centuries. She was the daughter of Costus, the governor of the Roman province of Alexandria. Although Christianity remained illegal under Roman rule, Catherine became one of its greatest proponents. According to Christian tradition, Catherine attempted to convince Roman Emperor Maximus to end the persecution of Christians. She did not convince him, but she did convert his wife and several other Roman philosophers. Eventually, Maximus had her imprisoned, and she was executed on the breaking wheel, a torture instrument that broke victims' limbs and eventually killed them. Catherine was named a martyr by the Orthodox Church, and later became one of the "Fourteen Holy Helpers" in the Roman Catholic Church. Emperor Justinian constructed Saint Catherine's Monastery at the foot of Mount Sinai in sixth-century Egypt. The monastery still exists today. Saint Catherine was also the visionary who spoke to and inspired Joan of Arc in the 15th century.

Songs that recognize the heritage of faith should be performed in a stately and reverent style. Still, some added repeated quarter notes or arpeggiated chords at the end of the poetic lines help keep singers from rushing ahead and perhaps increasing the tempo. Don't let the seriousness of the text cause you to take the tempo too slowly, though. Father's Day is a favorite time to use this song, or anytime the heritage of faith is celebrated.

Give Me That Old Time Religion *(page 50)*

This song is a standard hymn spiritual, popularized in the South by both African-American and Caucasian churches in the last quarter of the 19th century. It was the Fisk Jubilee Singers, an important group in modern hymnology, who transported this hymn from the workfield to the performance stage. In 1873, with the South still under martial law, Fisk University in Nashville needed additional funding for the education of newly freed men and women. The Jubilee Singers, already a well-known group, toured the United States and Europe raising money. The hymn "Give Me That Old Time Religion" was one of the songs published in the book *The Jubilee Singers and Their Campaign for Twenty Thousand Dollars.* Nearly 20 years later, Charlie D. Tillman, owner of a music publishing company, heard the song at an African-American tent revival in South Carolina. Without much regard for plagiarism or copyright, he scribbled the words on a scrap of paper and republished the tune in 1891, which was then distributed to a largely Caucasian audience. Using a little literary license, Tillman tampered with the lyrics, but the music was unchanged. Because this hymn appealed to everyone, it remains one of the foundational pieces of the southern gospel genre.

"Give Me That Old Time Religion" is a fun sing-along song, so you can be a little loose with the piano part. The primary role of the piano is to serve as a rhythm section with a bass line and chords to support the melody. The left hand should function like a string bass part and the right hand like a guitar or banjo. Some folks will probably know other verses to this song, so be ready to repeat as needed for the additional lyrics. This song is most often performed with *swing* eighths rather than *straight* eighths, so give it a *shuffle feel* as you play.

For an introduction, just start playing a *vamp* in G major. A vamp is just G major chords on beats two and four in the right-hand with the left hand playing G–D on beats one and three. You can use the first full measure repeated as an introduction. Either two bars or four bars will set up the tune.

God Be with You Till We Meet Again *(page 52)*

Jeremiah E. Rankin was certainly not afraid of cold weather. Born in New Hampshire in 1828, Rankin attended the prestigious Middlebury College in Vermont and later received graduate training from Andover Theological Seminary in Massachusetts. He must have grown tired of the long winters because he moved to Washington D.C. to lead the First Congregational Church. In 1889, Rankin became the President of Howard University, a prominent African-American college also located in the District of Columbia. After Rankin wrote the words to this hymn in 1880, he sent the lyrics to two different musicians. He later wrote, "The first stanza was written and sent to two composers — one of note, the other wholly unknown and not thoroughly educated in music. I selected the composition of the latter." William G. Tomer was a self-trained musician who served in the Union Army during the Civil War. He became the music director at the Grace Methodist Episcopal Church in Washington D.C. in the 1870s. This was his only published composition.

Years ago, many churches used this song as the final tune of departure from church services. It leaves people with a sense of anticipation at returning to meet again. It should be smooth and even in its performance style. It's not unusual for folks to put a short *fermata* or hold on the last "God" on the pick-up to the measure before the first ending, along with a natural *ritard*, or slowing tempo, going into the ending. The tempo goes back to normal on the repeated verses. If you want to get a laugh, pretend to announce mistakenly that we will sing, "God be with you till we *eat* again."

God of Our Fathers *(page 54)*

Daniel C. Roberts was a minister in rural New England in 1876. He wanted a hymn for his choir to perform for the local Centennial Celebration of the United States. So he wrote one himself. Roberts' hymn was published, and to his surprise the song became a hit. The hymn was widely performed throughout the region to celebrate the 100th anniversary of the signing of the Declaration of Independence. After 1876 a new musical composition was written to use specifically with the song. George William Warren was the composer of the tune that accompanies "God of Our Fathers." Warren was an organist extraordinaire who played for several churches in Albany and New York City. When he died in 1902 thousands attended his funeral, but the service excluded music. Friends and family believed that if they could "find no finer organist," then the absence of music would memorialize his musical legacy.

"God of Our Fathers" is indeed a dignified tune with a solid bass line and some trumpet-like fanfares to set it off. Play this song with a rich and full style. No need to worry about dynamic shadings. Build up to the final phrase of each verse as a climax to the hymn. You'll find other inspirational verses in most hymnbooks that you can use with this tune. This version of the song has included the "Amen." It is common practice to slow down on that last ending. All the triplet figures should be thought of as trumpet fanfare-type passages.

He Leadeth Me (page 60)

Joseph Gilmore was the son of the Governor of New Hampshire but passed up politics for a career in the ministry. Who can blame him? In 1862, as the War Between the States raged on, Gilmore led a special prayer service at the First Baptist Church in Philadelphia. Most Americans, North and South, believed in their side of the "cause," but after nearly two years of brutal war, both sides began to pray for divine guidance. After the service Joseph Gilmore jotted down some verses in his notebook and then went to bed. He soon forgot the words he had written, but his wife found them and sent them to the *Watchman and Reflector,* a Baptist periodical. Prominent musician William B. Bradbury saw Gilmore's verses and published them in his new hymnal *The Golden Censer.* In the spring of 1865, Gilmore walked to the pulpit to preach a trial sermon in Rochester, New York. When he opened the hymnal to select an opening chorus, the book opened to his hymn, "He Leadeth Me." Gilmore had had no idea his song had ever been read by anyone, let alone published and part of a hymnal.

Performance practices of many hymns vary from congregation to congregation in church use. As such, sometimes people become accustomed to adding fermatas to notes since they "grew up" singing a song in a particular way. So it is with "He Leadeth Me." Using the first verse as an example, many congregations in the past added a fermata of three beats (two extra beats) to the notes on the word "fraught" and the third "me" in the refrain. This arrangement adds the fermata on "me" at the end of the verse that is commonly performed. Other folks, however, have become accustomed to no fermatas at all in this hymn. Best advice: Go with the majority if it's a group. Do whatever you want if it's just you.

He's Got the Whole World in His Hands (page 57)

This chorus turned praise hymn is most likely taken from the book of John in the New Testament. Chapter 5, Verse 27 states, "and [the Father] has given him authority to execute judgment, because he is the Son of man." This song also reflects Chapter 5, Verse 19 in the book of Ephesians, "Speaking to yourselves in psalms and hymns and spiritual songs, singing and making melody in your heart to the Lord." The origins of the hymn are unknown but the song dates back to the spiritual genre of music that began in the late 19th century. In 1958, Laurie London released a new recording of the piece. Although Laurie is a common female name today, Laurie London was a very successful boy singer in England during the 1950s. It is the only gospel recording to ever hit #1 on the U.S. pop singles chart.

This arrangement has a "road map" (as some musicians call it), that can be confusing. Here's the navigation, because a GPS unit will do you no good. Start at the beginning and sing to the end of the first and second ending twice, going back to the repeat each time. The third time, skip the first and second ending and go to ending three. Go back to the same repeat. This time, when you get to the coda sign, skip to the coda. Or just forget all that and sing and play what sounds right to you. This song is most often performed with *swing* eighths. Keep a strong bass in the left hand.

Holy, Holy, Holy *(page 62)*

This hymn certainly emphasizes the Trinity. The lyrics were written by Reginald Heber and published posthumously by his widow and friends. He wrote the hymn in the early 1800s and used it specifically on Trinity Sunday each year. Trinity Sunday is celebrated eight weeks after Easter to reaffirm "God in three persons." In the 1860s, Dr. John B. Dykes wrote the music that is still used today. In sum, Dykes composed over 300 hymn tunes, but he created controversy in the Church of England by also writing music for non-Anglican hymns. In the 1956, 1975, and 1991 editions of the *Baptist Hymnal,* the song "Holy, Holy, Holy" is always easy to find; it is the very first hymn. You will be hard pressed to find any hymnbook or collection of traditional sacred songs that does not include "Holy, Holy, Holy." This tune has been around for a very long time.

Be steady and solid with all the parts. The left hand part is loaded with octaves, so if they get to be too much, you can just go with the lower notes. A *crescendo,* or increase in volume, up to the high E♭ in the melody will help highlight the climactic phrase of this hymn tune. Bring out any passing eighth notes.

I Have Decided to Follow Jesus *(page 68)*

The hymn "I Have Decided to Follow Jesus" has roots in British, American, and Indian history. The British Empire gained and maintained control over parts of India in the 19th and 20th centuries. Because of this, missionary groups primarily from Britain and the United States enjoyed greater access to the region. As the number of missionaries grew, so did the number of Indians who converted to Christianity. The Garo tribe had lived for centuries in the state of Meghalaya, which borders the Himalayas. The individual composer of this song is unknown, but the tune evolved from the Garo tribe of Northeastern India. Garo Indians also wrote the lyrics of the hymn. Sources suggest that S. Sundar Singh, Ramke W. Momin, and/or Obed W. Momin wrote the song after converting to Christianity. Early versions of the hymn were simply entitled, "Hindustani Melody." The Free Methodist Church in Indiana first published it in the U.S. in 1950.

This lovely devotional song is often used at the close of meetings. Keep it understated in rhythm and dynamic level. It should be played in a two beat per bar feel. A *ritard,* or slowdown on the last verse before the final ending is appropriate, along with a *decrescendo* in dynamic level. This tune is simple, so keep the performance simple as well.

I Know That My Redeemer Lives *(page 70)*

This hymn was written in 1775 just before the American colonies declared independence. Samuel Medley had just begun his ministry in Herefordshire, England when these words came to him while preparing for a sermon. He wrote 20 hymns before his death in 1799. The music associated with this hymn was not added until the 1790s. The actual name of the tune is "Duke Street," named for the composer's residence in Windle, Lancaster, England. Little is known about the composer, John Hatton, except that according to legend he was killed after being thrown from a stagecoach.

This song is a joyous yet stately celebration of the Easter resurrection. Keep the tempo moderate and it's okay to be a little heavy-handed. On the whole notes, you can help retain the time and mood if you just repeat the left hand bass notes. There are several other verses to this hymn that can be found in many hymnals. Consider using the last four bars of the song for an introduction. This particular tune is also used a lot for the text "Jesus Shall Reign Where'er the Sun."

In the Garden (page 65)

Places in the Heart hit movie theatres in 1984, and featured an all-star cast including Sally Fields, Danny Glover, John Malkovich, and Ed Harris. The film earned two Oscars® and numerous other film awards. Set in Texas in 1935, the movie tells the story of Edna Spalding (Sally Fields), recently widowed, who is determined to save her home by producing the season's first crop of cotton. The hymn "In the Garden" is featured prominently in the film, but the movie's plot — full of blood, sweat, and tears — is anything but a walk in the garden. Yet, as the lyrics of the hymn suggest, faith helps the farm survive in the wake of sorrow and hard times. C. Austin Miles wrote the words and music for this hymn in 1912. His inspiration was taken from the Gospel of John, and Miles himself claimed to have had a vision of Mary Magdalene and Jesus. He immediately wrote the words and added the music the following day. Miles served for 37 years as the editor and manager of the gospel publishing house Hall-Mack. This song is one of the most popular hymns of all time. It tells a story of an encounter with Christ in a beautiful garden.

"In the Garden" is traditionally played in A♭, with some very nice harmony to support a lyrical melodic line. This arrangement keeps the accompaniment very simple for the verse with some nice flowing eighth notes in the right hand for the chorus. When you get to the chorus, let your left hand play the notes that have the stems down in the treble clef. Toward the end, the left hand goes back to the bass clef. Often singers will put a short fermata (or hold) on the words "other" and "ever." In fact, you can just about count on that. People love this song as a solo or with a group.

It Is Well with My Soul (page 72)

The story of Horatio G. Spafford, author of "It Is Well with My Soul," is a compelling one. Spafford had achieved the American dream after becoming a successful lawyer in Chicago with a loving wife and five children. His dream quickly unraveled. The Great Chicago Fire of 1871 claimed his real estate investments and his only son died of illness. In 1873, Spafford decided the family needed an extended vacation and chose a European tour. Business kept him from traveling with his family, and their ship sank after crashing into a British vessel named the *Lochearn*. Spafford's four daughters were drowned, and his wife sent a telegraph that read, "Saved alone." He wrote this hymn in his grief as he prayed for guidance and strength. The line, "When sorrows like sea billows roll" speaks of the loss of his daughters. In a strange turn of events, Spafford and his wife had two more children and moved to Jerusalem in 1881. They established the American Colony in Israel as a Christian ministry. He died in 1889 of malaria. The family's story is recounted by their daughter, Bertha Spafford Vesper, in her book *Our Jerusalem*.

Take the stylistic term *peacefully* to heart when performing this well-known hymn. Keep the tempo moderate to allow the message of the text to be fully expressed. A smooth bass line and even chords will provide the appropriate musical context. Begin to build with a *crescendo,* or increasing volume, at the top of the second page as the melody ascends. Begin backing off with the title line "It is well" that rounds out the verse each time. Since there are four verses, you can use the introduction as an interlude to give some relief to the singers' voices.

Jesus, Keep Me Near the Cross (page 74)

This hymn is another Fanny Crosby favorite. However, this song involved two additional blockbuster musicians of the hymn world. William Batchelder Bradbury wrote and edited 59 volumes of religious and secular songs. Most churchgoers have seen his work, although his name is typically written Wm. B. Bradbury when given credit. Bradbury was instrumental in the Sunday School movement, and many of his publications are for children. His most famous piece is "Jesus Loves Me." He was working on another compilation when he died in 1868. *Bright Jewels for the Sunday School* was published posthumously in 1869 and contained Crosby's hymn "Jesus, Keep Me Near the Cross." William Howard Doane composed the music for this hymn, and he partnered with Fanny Crosby on several hymn compositions. Doane was also a high roller of hymnology with over 2,000 tunes, including "To God Be the Glory." Despite his musical success, Doane paid the bills by way of his full-time job as president of an Ohio woodworking machinery company.

"Jesus, Keep Me Near the Cross" is a lovely, gently flowing hymn tune with a beautiful text. It should be performed in an easy *two-feel* to each bar. Add some *arpeggiated* eighth notes to the right hand on some of the dotted quarter notes and some repeated eighths occasionally in the left hand. Increase the dynamic level on the chorus to heighten the poetic climax with a dynamic decrease on the last two measures. The musical term for that is *morendo*, dying away. Often the third verse is skipped for reasons of length and endurance.

Jesus, Thou Joy of Loving Hearts *(page 76)*

Martin Luther remains a significant figure in Christianity. After all, he did instigate the greatest divide in Christianity with his *Ninety-Five Theses* (1517), which set the Protestant Reformation into motion. Luther thought very highly of a Roman Catholic abbot named Bernard of Clairvaux who lived in 12th-century France. Bernard wrote the words of "Jesus, Thou Joy of Loving Hearts," but it was probably his involvement with church politics that earned him adoration in the eyes of Luther. Saint Bernard was the monk who chose between two competing popes in the Great Schism of 1130. He also led reform efforts in the Cistercian monastic order, organized the Second Crusade (which failed to conquer Jerusalem), and founded 163 monasteries throughout Europe. Pope Alexander III canonized Bernard of Clairvaux in 1174. Ray Palmer translated the hymn from Latin to English in 1858.

This song has five verses with the same melody, like most hymns, but this arrangement has a *modulation,* or a change of key, to F major for the fifth verse. This brings new emphasis and energy to the final verse, keeping things interesting for both the listener and performer. If you just want to perform two or three of the first verses, take the fourth ending whenever you are ready. Prepare for the new key signature. You lose two flats when going to the key of F, which is a friendly key — and the melody is still in a very reasonable range. You can increase the volume level on the final verse. It remains a lovely melody and text.

Just a Closer Walk with Thee *(page 78)*

This hymn is undoubtedly linked with southern culture, gospel music, and covered dish dinners. Elvis Presley recorded this hymn in 1956, setting record sales. Country music legend Randy Travis recorded it in 2003 and re-released it on another album in 2009. It has been recorded by over 100 artists and remains a standard tune for traditional New Orleans jazz funerals. Its author is unknown, but this hymn also grew from the spiritual tradition of African-Americans in the early 20th century. The Selah Jubilee Singers, a choir group associated with Raleigh, North Carolina, first recorded "Just a Closer Walk with Thee" in 1941. The group was also the first gospel choir to perform at the famed Apollo Theater.

A definite *shuffle-feel* for this popular sing-along song is most appropriate. If the piece is sung by a soloist, some individual expression with the rhythm and melodic line is just fine. The road map for this song is to take the first ending, go back to the chorus, then the second ending, back to the chorus, before taking the coda, which goes to a short ending on the second page. If you want to repeat the last line for an extended ending, you won't be the first to do it, so perform as the Spirit leads.

Just as I Am (page 107)

The story behind the hymn is lovely. Different versions of the story exist, but it began with Charlotte Elliott, a sickly young woman living in Brighton, England. Elliott's health deteriorated, and by the age of 30, she was virtually bedridden. After visiting with the Swiss evangelist Dr. César Malan, Elliott converted to Christianity and dedicated her life to Christ. The next year Elliott wrote a poem meant to comfort other invalids who also felt helpless and lonely. She sent the poem to a publisher and hoped that any proceeds would go to her brother's school, St. Margaret's Hall in Brighton. In 1836, Elliott published a book of hymns entitled *The Invalid's Hymn Book,* which contained 115 original works. William B. Bradbury wrote the tune associated with "Just as I Am" in 1849. Her brother, Reverend Henry V. Elliott wrote of his paralyzed sister, "In the course of a long ministry, I hope I have been permitted to see some of the fruit of my labor, but I feel that far more has been done by a single hymn of my sister's."

"Just as I Am" is frequently used as a song of commitment. Being a reflective text, the music should reinforce the emotion of commitment with a smooth and even performance. One decision that needs to be made is whether to sing or play the song with two beats per bar with a dotted half note as the beat, or six beats per bar with a quarter note receiving one beat. Either way is fine, but don't take the tempo too fast. You'll find additional lyrics for other verses in hymnals everywhere.

Kum Ba Yah (page 108)

The hymn "Kum Ba Yah" conjures images of eating s'mores around a campfire. Ethnomusicologists believe that this sing-along emerged in the 1920s in either South Carolina or Georgia near the Atlantic coastline. In the early 1930s the Society for the Preservation of Spirituals collected this tune, which was sung "Come By Yuh." Reportedly, the song originated with former slaves who spoke in Gullah, a Creole dialect. Thus, the hymn's title is most likely a derivative of its literal translation "come by here." The Reverend Marvin V. Frey claimed to have written the song in 1936 and claimed the copyrights, and subsequent royalties, from the hymn's success. However, the Gullah version was recorded nearly 20 years earlier.

If there were ever a tune that was made popular from campfire sing-alongs, this is it. This arrangement is in 3/4 time rather than the more commonly used 4/4 time. You could quite easily add a fourth beat to each bar, but 3/4 will work just fine. Imagine a strumming guitar for the accompaniment with a nice sustained bass line. The humming of the repeat of the last musical phrase along with a slowing of the tempo will make a nice close to any sing-along, with or without a campfire.

Leaning on the Everlasting Arms (page 112)

This tried-and-true gospel tune was written in 1887 and published in *The Glad Evangel for Revival, Camp, and Evangelistic Meetings.* Elisha Hoffman is credited as the song's author, but the hymn was published, in part, because of his connection with Anthony J. Showalter. Showalter started working on the hymn after hearing of the death of two friends. He wrote some of the words and composed a tune, but Showalter needed help to finish. He called on Elisha A. Hoffman, who finished the lyrics and chorus of "Leaning on the Everlasting Arms." Luckily for Hoffman, Showalter happened to own a publishing business, A.J. Showalter & Company. Hoffman went on to write over 2,000 gospel songs and edited 50 songbooks.

Tessitura is a musical term that is used to describe the general range of a song. "Leaning on the Everlasting Arms" in this arrangement has a high *tessitura.* You'll need to use some vocal energy to sing all those Ds. Also, there are some three-note chords in the left hand where you may be more accustomed to playing a single note. If it's more comfortable, that will work. This song is usually performed in a march-like fashion, with crisp and clean dotted eighths and six-teenths. As is the case with many hymns, you can easily find additional verses that are familiar to many people in hymnals of any number of Protestant denominations. Because there's no written-out introduction, the last two bars of the song will work just fine to set the tempo and give the pitch.

Lift Ev'ry Voice and Sing (page 109)

"Lift Ev'ry Voice and Sing" is often called "The Black National Anthem," but like many hymns, it began as a poem. James Weldon Johnson wrote the poem, and his brother, John R. Johnson, set it to music in 1905. Students at the Stanton School, where James Johnson served as princi-pal, first performed the poem publicly in 1900 on February 12th — Abraham Lincoln's birth-day. The poem was specifically used to introduce the celebration's guest speaker, Booker T. Washington. As the 20th century progressed, the song grew in popularity and inspired hope in the face of continued discrimination and violence against African-Americans. In 1919, the National Association for the Advancement of Colored Persons (NAACP) adopted it as their organizational anthem. By the 1920s, the song was pasted into the hymnals of most African-American churches. James Johnson was an amazing man. He received his Bachelor's degree at Atlanta University, served as principal of the Stanton School (his high school Alma Mater), composed hundreds of songs for Broadway plays, practiced law in Florida, served as a United States Consul in both Venezuela and Nicaragua, taught creative writing at Fisk University, and wrote and published *The Autobiography of an Ex-Coloured Man* (1912). He died in 1938 at the age of 67.

This song has one of those heavy beats to it. Keep the tempo moderate so that the lyrics will be fully understood. Each beat has three eighth notes in it. Some added repeated chords in the right hand will keep the tempo from rushing ahead. Another factor to consider is the *tessitura,* or general pitch range of the song. This tune goes up to a high G several times and stays in the moderately high range quite a bit. On those places with the high notes, the piano player should play with firm and strong confidence. It will help the singers use enough air to reach those high notes.

The Lord Bless You and Keep You (page 114)

Nineteenth-century evangelist and publisher Dwight Moody wrote of this hymn, "Here is a benediction that can be given all the time without being impoverished. Every heart may utter it, every letter may conclude with it, every day may begin with it, every night may be sancti-fied by it. . . . It is the Lord Himself who [gives us] this bar of music from heaven's infinite anthem." Peter Christian Lutkin wrote the music and words of "The Lord Bless You and Keep You" in the mid-1800s. Lutkin was a composer and conductor who studied extensively in Europe. He was a highly acclaimed organist in Chicago, Illinois, and in 1895 he founded the School of Music at Northwestern University.

This song is found in the "Service Music" section included in many traditional hymnals. The music in those sections includes things like prayer responses, calls to worship, and some benedictions. This arrangement calls for two voices, and it could easily use multiple singers on each part. It has a very active accompaniment, with a moving left hand and a variety of rhythms in the right hand. If things get too complicated for the piano player, here are some suggestions. In the left hand, play just the first notes on beats one and three in each bar and sustain them. In the right hand the top notes are the main melody, so just play them if you can't get everything in that's written. This piece may need more practice than others.

The Lord's My Shepherd, I'll Not Want (page 116)

This hymn is typically not associated with good times. Used as a common hymn for funerals, it is based on the 23rd Psalm, "The Lord is my Shepherd, I shall not want. He maketh me lie down in green pastures; he leads me beside quiet waters." The complete lyrics were first written in 17th-century Scotland, a land full of green pastures and surrounded by water. Jessie S. Irvine, also a Scotsman, wrote the music and entitled the piece "Crimond." Several earlier musical accompaniments associated with this hymn are still used in Scotland and England. They include: George T. Smart's "Wiltshire" (1795), Hugh Wilson's "Martyrdom" (1800), John Campbell's "Orlington" (1807), William Gardiner's "Belmont" (1812), and William H. Havergal's "Evan" (1847).

This melody has a long history and has a timeless folk-song quality to it. The chord changes are fluid and natural, so keep an easy tempo flowing throughout. A few *chromatics* (added sharps and flats) can be found, but they don't really add to the difficulty of the piece. Let the piano imitate the sound of a guitar with finger-picking. The song has five verses and all are important, because it is a paraphrase of the 23rd Psalm.

Love Lifted Me (page 118)

Country singer and entertainer Kenny Rogers remains famous for his song and album entitled *The Gambler,* which won him a GRAMMY® for Best Male Country Vocal Performance in 1980. Rogers later cut an album entitled "Love Lifted Me" that included an adaptive version of this hymn. Ironically, Kenny Rogers isn't the only "gambling" reference for this hymn history. The hymn's author, James Rowe, gambled big on his future. With a little money in his pocket, the 24-year-old Rowe jumped on a boat and immigrated to the United States in 1889. Between 1880 and 1930, over 27 million people entered the United States with approximately 20 million coming through Ellis Island. Rowe was cleared through Ellis Island and worked in the railroad yards of New York. He had always possessed a knack for words and music, and so he moved to Texas and then Tennessee to pursue a career in the music publishing industry. Rowe wrote this hymn based on the parable of Jesus and Peter on Lake Tiberius. As Jesus walked on the water he bid Peter to join him. Peter stepped out of the boat and started walking toward Jesus, but as the wind grew so did Peter's fear. He began to sink and cried out for help. Jesus stretched out his hand and "love lifted" Peter out of the windy waters.

Musicians sometimes use the term *liltingly* to describe the style of a song like "Love Lifted Me." It implies a light, easy swing feel. Usually songs that are performed *liltingly* are in a simple compound meter like 6/8. That means that there are two beats in the measure and each quarter note beat is divided into three eighth notes. Keep the tempo moderate and build up to the chorus "Love lifted me." Traditionally, a *ritard,* or slowing down, is used on the line "When nothing else could help" and a *fermata,* or hold, on "Love" and the second syllable of "lifted" in the next-to-last measure. That helps to emphasize the main lyrical idea on a musical high note. If you want to have a little fun with this tune, have people stand on their toes whenever they sing the word "lifted."

A Mighty Fortress Is Our God (page 120)

"A Mighty Fortress Is Our God" is Reformation leader Martin Luther's greatest contribution to Christian hymnody. In fact, it is also called the "Battle Hymn of the Reformation," and its first line is inscribed on Luther's tomb in Wittenberg, Germany. Written in 1529, this hymn is nearly 500 years old, but the music associated with it wasn't added until the 1800s. It has been translated over 60 times for use in hymnals and into different languages. Martin Luther loved music and studied Gregorian chant in his training as a monk, but he was discouraged by the lack of participation allowed churchgoers, including congregational singing. After his excommunication from the Catholic Church, Luther specifically spoke of the importance of music in church:

"Music and theology alone are capable of giving peace and happiness to troubled souls." Luther's influence solidified the prominent place of music in Protestant denominations that continues today.

This song is a serious text with a sturdy tune that needs a deliberate touch. Every phrase ends with a *fermata,* or hold, so there is no need to hurry through this tune. Because it moves so slowly, an added octave in the left hand adds some weight to the performance. You'll notice that only the first two verses are printed beneath the music, with two additional verses printed separately at the end of the song. The tune is familiar and many singers will be able to sing the verse without even looking at the music. Martin Luther's intent was to write music that the common person could sing and enjoy in their native language, or *vernacular.* This is his most famous piece. To begin this hymn, just have the piano player play a C major chord and go.

My Faith Looks Up to Thee *(page 122)*

In 1835, Ray Palmer and Lowell Mason met in the streets of Boston. Palmer was a recent graduate of Yale University, and Mason was on his way to earning a Doctorate of Music. Although both would become well-known musicians and theologians, these two men certainly didn't enter their professional careers in the music business. Palmer started as a clerk for a dry goods shop, and Mason began as a bank teller. Mason wrote in the 1820s, "I was then a bank officer in Savannah, and did not wish to be known as a musical man, as I had not the least thought of ever making music a profession." However, by 1835 both men were making a name for themselves in the Boston church circuit. Mason directed three choirs and had just compiled his first collection of music entitled *Spiritual Songs for Social Worship.* In the same year, Palmer was ordained as a Congregational minister. As they met on the street that fateful day, Mason stopped Palmer and asked him to write a few verses for a song he was working on. Their collaboration, "My Faith Looks Up to Thee" remains one of the most recognizable and cherished hymns of the 19th and 20th centuries.

This song has a nice, smooth flowing text. With four verses of descriptive language and a simple accompaniment, try using a different dynamic level for each verse. Here's a suggestion: Sing verse one at a *mezzo-forte* (or moderately loud) level, verse two at a *mezzo-piano* (or moderately soft) level, the third verse at a *piano* (or soft) level, and verse four at a *forte* (or loud) level. This variation will make the intensity of the song grow to the final verse for emphasis. Another suggestion is to have a soloist sing one verse, probably verse three.

Nearer, My God, to Thee *(page 124)*

This hymn originated with an actress turned writer in 1837. Sarah Flower Adams traded in the lines of Lady Macbeth (her final role) for a different kind of lyrical drama. From 1837 until her death in 1848 Adams published poems, articles, hymns, and a children's catechism book entitled *The Flock at the Fountain* (1845). Lowell Mason (see "My Faith Looks Up to Thee") put Adams' verses for "Nearer, My God, to Thee" to music in 1856 and the hymn became very popular in England. The hymn is based loosely on Chapter 28 in the Book of Genesis. However, Adams never could have guessed the symbolism that "Nearer, My God, to Thee" holds today. The hymn is associated with the calm that one experiences just before death, and two major historical tragedies solidified its reputation as a "dying prayer." In 1901, United States President William McKinley was assassinated, and he whispered the song's lyrics as he lay dying. As part of his memorial, every city in America observed a moment of silence and then sang "Nearer, My God, to Thee." In 1912, the luxury liner *Titanic* struck an iceberg. Although disputed by some, many surviving passengers claimed that the ship's orchestra played the hymn as it sank into the Atlantic. In 1980, shortly before the launch of the CNN news network in Atlanta, owner Ted Turner promised that barring technical problems, "We won't be signing off until the world ends . . . and when the end of the world comes, we'll play 'Nearer, My God, to Thee' before we sign off."

If a singer is involved, or even if this song is performed by solo piano, an introduction is in order. The standard introduction when there isn't one written is the last four bars of the song. That works great here. An introduction does a couple of things. It establishes the key or starting note, and it also sets the mood and tempo for the performance. Keep the tempo moderately slow with a steady bass part in the left hand. If the piano voicing in the right hand in bar 10 is hard to reach, just leave out the bottom note. Nobody will miss it.

O Perfect Love (page 126)

"O Perfect Love" is a hymn of happiness. It remains one of the most often played hymns for weddings. The tune was composed by Joseph Barnby and is also called "Sandringham" in some hymnals. The original words were part of a hymn entitled "Strength and Stay" until Dorothy Blomfield Gurney's sister decided that she wanted the song for her wedding. In 1883, on a typical Sunday night at the Blomfield house, family members read, played, and sang for their evening entertainment. After singing "Strength and Stay" Dorothy's recently engaged sister turned and said, "What is the use of a sister who composes poetry if she cannot write new words to a favorite tune? I would like to use the tune at my wedding." Dorothy replied, "If no one will disturb me, I will go into the library and see what I can do." Within fifteen minutes she was back with the group and reading the words she had jotted down. The hymn was a hit, and in 1892 Queen Victoria knighted Joseph Barnby, the tune's composer, for his many musical contributions to Great Britain.

This song has a beautiful melody with a clean, flowing accompaniment. The left hand part in this arrangement is rather active and often wide-spread, covering larger *intervals,* or distances between notes. In the first measure, the left hand part is A♭, E♭, and C, covering the interval of a tenth — that's an octave and a third. This may be a stretch, especially for someone with smaller hands. You can substitute an A♭, an octave above the first note in the left hand, instead of middle C. This song is frequently used for weddings, so it's a good tune to have ready when called upon.

The Old Rugged Cross (page 128)

Even Merle Haggard could not resist singing this hymn. He recorded it on his 1994 album "What a Friend We Have in Jesus." In fact, almost every legendary country singer has recorded the song including Patsy Cline, Chet Atkins, Johnny Cash, and Loretta Lynn. George Bennard wrote the words and music for "The Old Rugged Cross" in 1913. The hymn was published in 1915, popularized by the Billy Sunday evangelistic campaigns of the 1920s, and first recorded by Virginia Asher and Homer Rodeheaver in 1921. The three small towns of Albion, Michigan; Pokagon, Michigan; and Sturgeon Bay, Wisconsin all claim to be the birthplace of the hymn. To add a little more competition to the mix, Reed City, Michigan maintains a museum dedicated to the life and ministry of George Bennard.

Although most published versions of "The Old Rugged Cross" are in a 6/8 meter, this arrangement is in 3/4, which is the way the song is generally perceived. Use a *swing feel* in a moderate tempo and let the vocals be free in their interpretation. This song is much loved, and it can be an effective solo or group song. Build up to the closing line "I will cling to the old rugged cross." A *ritard,* or slowing down on the last verse is an appropriate way to close out the song. Or, repeating the last line, "And exchange it someday for a crown," is a good way to conclude the song. Other verses can be readily found in just about any hymnal.

Only Trust Him (page 134)

John Hart Stockton, composer of "Down at the Cross" and "Just as I Am," also wrote the words and music for this hymn. The original title of the song is "Come, Every Soul by Sin Oppressed." Stockton accompanied Mr. Dwight L. Moody, minister, educator, and founder of the Moody Bible Institute, on a trip to England in 1873. As they traveled across the Atlantic, Stockton perused his notebook of hymns. He came across "Come, Every Soul by Sin Oppressed" and later wrote, "Believing that these words had been so often sung that they were hackneyed, I decided to change them and tell how to come to Jesus by substituting the words, 'Only trust him.'" Stockton used the word "hackneyed" to mean lacking in freshness or originality, and he certainly freshened up this hymn. He rewrote his own words based on the Book of John, Chapter 14, "Do not let your hearts be troubled. Trust in God; trust also in Me." The new version of the song was published in 1884 as part of his *Salvation Melodies* collection.

Because this arrangement has no written-out introduction, you can create one. The natural introduction for most songs is the last four bars, and that is the case here. Start three bars before the first ending on the first "He will save you," take the first ending and then start on verse one. This song should be understated throughout. Keep the volume down and don't let the tempo get too fast. It's an appeal, not a forceful statement, so keep that in mind. If you play it as a solo, repeating the line "He will save you now" at the end will create an effective close to the tune.

Onward, Christian Soldiers (page 131)

The Salvation Army adopted this hymn as one of its processionals, which makes perfect sense. Both the song and the organization harbor images of "muscular Christianity," and hold out the idea that religion and patriotism remain inextricably linked. This belief literally characterizes Christians as a "religious infantry" ready to fight in the name of God and country. Great Britain and the United States have long stood as powerful nations, and both countries maintain a strong tradition of Protestantism. In 1941, Winston Churchill and Franklin D. Roosevelt met on the battleship *HMS Prince of Wales* to sign the Atlantic Charter. Afterward, the group sang the hymn "Onward, Christian Soldiers" at a church service held aboard the ship. Churchill explained his choice of songs in a radio broadcast on the BBC: "We sang 'Onward, Christian Soldiers' indeed, and I felt that this was no vain presumption, but that we had the right to feel that we were serving a cause for the sake of which a trumpet has sounded from on high. When I looked upon that densely packed congregation of fighting men . . . it swept across me that here was the only hope, but also the sure hope, of saving the world from measureless degradation."

Sabine Baring-Gould originally penned the song in 1854. The Englishman wrote the song for the post-Easter Whitmonday celebration. The celebration included a large group of children carrying crosses and banners, who marched from Horbury, England to the next town. He wrote the hymn for them to sing as they marched. Baring-Gould also wrote over 100 novels and other works. Some Protestant denominations have challenged this hymn because of what they perceive as its overt militarism.

This hymn is indeed in a march style, but the traditional march tempo of 120 beats per minute isn't required. Instead, go with something a little slower, say 116 beats per minute, so the lyrics are well projected and not rushed. To simulate a bass, you could keep quarter notes going in the left hand. This song is actually pitched a little low, so do your best to keep the melody projected on notes below middle C. Don't slow down at the end of this one. Keep the tempo steady right through to the end. Be accurate with the pronunciation on this wordy text.

Precious Memories *(page 136)*

John Braselton Fillmore Wright, better known as J.B.F. Wright, authored and composed the hymn "Precious Memories." Wright was born in Tennessee in 1877 and served as a member in the Church of God. He was a self-taught musician who had little formal training. However, the inspiration for this hymn didn't require a highbrow education; it came straight from the heart. After years of "rambling over Texas," Wright and his wife settled in Cisco, Texas. He took a job as the custodian and nurseryman for Cisco Junior College. In the summer of 1923, his youngest son died of diphtheria, and the Wright family was devastated. Everett, the son, had been a charismatic little fellow who loved to wave at the trainmen as they passed by on a railroad track that ran beside their house. After his son's death, Wright watched as trains passed with workers waving and looking for Everett. His grief and fond memories of Everett led him to write this hymn. In sum, Wright wrote over 500 hymns, but this remains his biggest hit. The song even touched Bob Dylan who recorded it on his album *Knocked Out Loaded* (1986).

This old timey funeral song is also a sentimental look at life and the events of childhood and growing older. This setting is done in a blues style with lots of seventh chords that give it a blues flavor. It's a shuffle, so give every beat the triplet feel. The left hand has many octaves, so if that is too much to cover, just go with a single bass note. You'll also find some little *grace notes* in the right hand. These will make the accompaniment sound in the *Floyd Cramer* style. Floyd Cramer was a popular piano player in the 1960s who was known for his use of grace notes. Keep the tempo on the moderate to slow side and let the singers be free in their stylistic interpretation. Adding a group of voices on the chorus, with a soloist on the verses, is a nice touch.

Rock of Ages *(page 140)*

This hymn is based on the Psalms passage "The Lord is my Rock, and my Fortress, and my Deliverer," but there is more to the story. Some legends claim that Augustus M. Toplady, a Calvinist minister in London, wrote the words amidst a storm in 1776. A different account of the hymn's genesis is that it was born from a disagreement between the author and John Wesley, both Reformation ministers and leaders. The most humorous story associated with this hymn occurred sometime in the 19th or early 20th century. A British missionary in India wanted to translate this hymn into the native dialect, and hired a young Hindu Bible student. The translation came back, "Very old stone, split for my benefit; Let me absent myself under one of your fragments."

 As with many tunes, a stylistic decision needs to be made regarding the performance of this well-known tune. One style is the traditional straight-feeling rhythm. In that style, the dotted eighths and sixteenth figures are crisp and clean, and the eighth notes even and smooth. Another stylistic interpretation is to swing the eighth notes and give every beat a triplet feel. This way the beats with two eighth notes and the dotted eighth and sixteenths sound the same. A good ending for the last verse is to repeat the last phrase, "Let me hide myself in Thee" with a slowing tempo. Keep the bass in the left hand solid to move the piece along. The performance tempo could range widely from slow to moderate, depending on the mood of the performers, so be flexible in that regard.

Simple Gifts *(page 142)*

It is no coincidence that this hymn contains the word "simple" in its title. The Shaker community was known for simple living, dancing, and music, but not many of their songs have broken into mainstream hymnology. Future chances for musical stardom are also slim, considering only three practicing Shakers live in the United States today. The Shakers first appeared in 1747 England under the guidance of Mother Ann Lee. The group splintered from the Quakers, and both groups hold the belief that serving God is best accomplished through personal dedication and an environment of simple, moral living. Shakers believed that clergymen and religious rituals were unnecessary. However, this Christian group did not simply worship together; they lived together as well. The author of "Simple Gifts" was Elder Joseph Brackett from Maine. Brackett wrote the song in 1848 as a Shaker spiritual and dance song. Interestingly, the Shakers created a form of music notation that used letters instead of notes. A musical staff was rarely used, and rhythmic patterns were written in short notation. The hymn achieved worldwide notoriety after American composer Aaron Copland arranged the tune for *Appalachian Spring* (1944) and *Old American Songs* (1950).

If you're a pianist who prefers flats to sharps, don't hesitate to play this arrangement in E♭ major, with three flats, instead of E major with four sharps. Just read the notes as they are and play everything in E♭ major. The left hand has a lot of rocking eighth notes, so if there is a fatigue factor, you can just play the notes on the beats as quarter notes. Because this is a fairly short arrangement you can give it more length by repeating back to the verse with just the piano playing solo. Bring the voice or voices back in on the line, "When true simplicity is gained," and finish out the tune. A *ritard,* or slowing down, on the last two bars along with a *decrescendo,* or decrease in volume, will put a nice touch on the ending of the song.

Stand Up, Stand Up for Jesus (page 144)

Dudley A. Tyng was a man born to preach. The apple didn't fall far from the tree because Dudley's father, Stephen, was also a prominent minister in Philadelphia. In 1858, the younger Tyng delivered a sermon to over 5,000 people attending "The Work of God in Philadelphia" revival. The next week, Tyng was hard at work in his study and decided to take a break. He wandered out to the barn where a mule was powering a machine used to thresh corn. According to a family friend, Tyng walked over to the mule and and got his sleeve caught in the cog of the wheel. As a result, Tyng's arm was severely lacerated and the bleeding could not be stopped. His father heard the news and rushed to his son's side. As Dudley Tyng took his last breath he told his father, "Tell them to stand up for Jesus." After his death, fellow minister George Duffield wrote the words of this hymn as a poetic memorial for his fallen friend. However, the lyrics were so powerful that one of his parishioners had the poem reprinted as a Sunday School leaflet. A Baptist periodical picked up the words, giving the hymn an even wider audience.

It's a standard inside joke for a congregation to say that it's in their church constitution that you can't sing this song while seated. This song is a good march-style hymn, so take it at a march tempo and hold it steady throughout. There is no introduction, so try opening it up with repeated G major chords in tempo with a G octave in the left hand in straight quarter notes to set the tempo and the mood. You can find additional verses in many hymnals. This song is a great opener for a meeting if you need one, and it's a super group sing-along tune.

Sweet By and By (page 146)

This hymn is a gospel classic and is commonly used for funerals. However, it was not written for a funeral, but rather was composed after a friendly conversation at the drug store. The author, Sanford Bennett, owned a drug store in Elkhorn, Wisconsin. One day at work, Joseph Webster, the town's most prominent musician, stopped by looking rather melancholy. As the story goes, Bennett asked Webster what was the trouble and Webster replied, "It will be all right by and by." Bennett thought his words poetic and scribbled some verses on a piece of paper behind the counter. He showed the words to Webster and asked, "Why would that not make a good hymn?" Webster wrote some notes, pulled out his violin (a must-have when going to the drug store), and began playing the melody we know today. Bennett later wrote, "It was not over thirty minutes from the time I took my pen to write the words before two friends with Webster and myself were singing the hymn." It is Bennett's only hymn, but Webster wrote over 1,000 musical compositions.

Also known by the title, "There's a Land That Is Fairer Than Day," this is a tune and text that many folks who grew up in a traditional church will know very well. Though it speaks of heaven, the song isn't associated with the usual funeral tragedy, but is rather a joyous expression of anticipation of what is to come.

 Sing and play with a little bounce. Keep the eighth notes even and the dotted eighths and sixteenths crisp and clean. Some "echo chords" on the chorus respond to the main melody. If a group is singing this song, part of the group could echo the words with the piano. As usual, a repeat of the last phrase, "We shall meet on that beautiful shore," brings the tune to an appropriate close.

Sweet Hour of Prayer (page 148)

Hymnologists have William B. Bradbury to thank for this song (for more of his work, see "He Leadeth Me" and "Jesus, Keep Me Near the Cross). This hymn was composed by Bradbury and popularized through one of his 59 published compilations. However, Bradbury didn't write the words. The lyrics originated with an unlikely source, a blind artisan in the small town of Coleshill, England. William Walford owned a small trinket shop where he sold his wood and bone carvings. In 1842, Reverend Thomas Salmon visited the shop, and Walford asked if he could dictate some lines. Salmon wrote down the words as Walford recited them. Three years later, Reverend Salmon submitted the poem to the *New York Observer.* In 1859, William B. Bradbury ran across a copy of the poem and instantly saw its potential as a hymn. He wrote the accompaniment and published it in his *Cottage Melodies.* Walford passed away in 1850, never to know of the song's success.

This song is one of the most popular devotional hymns in the hymnody. Even though it is written in 6/8 it really has the feel of two three-beat measures in every bar, so relax and don't ever rush through this one. You'll find some stretched hand positions at the beginning of the first verse, which is tough for folks with small hands and creates some fingering problems. Don't feel that you have to play every note. Leave out the lower octave and just play the two top notes. The song will sound fine and be easier to play. There is a natural *ritard* going into the *fermata* before the first ending. Slow down and build up the volume. In the musical world we sometimes say, *"Milk it,"* meaning be extra expressive; especially on the last verse as the line is, "And shout while passing through the air." Talk about a dramatic line!

Take My Life and Let It Be (page 141)

Frances Ridley Havergal lived in constant sickness and physical frailty, but she persevered with her faith in one hand and a pen in the other. In 1874, Havergal attended a party in England, and later that evening found herself restless and unable to sleep. She arose and wrote the words for "Take My Life and Let It Be." She had finished the final draft by sunrise. The verse "Take my silver and my gold; Not a mite would I withhold" holds particular significance. Havergal was a firm believer in humility and generosity. In 1878, she donated most of her possessions to a local charity.

Because this hymn is really in the form of a prayer, keep it simple and on the quiet side. All the verses are good, but things get a little monotonous just singing the same tune four times. Instead, use the introduction as an interlude after the verses. It will give the voices time to rest a little and break up the continuous sound of the song. If anything, make the last verse a little slower and more deliberate to bring finality to the hymn. This hymn is perfect to use for missionary, deacon, pastoral, or other commissioning services, since it is all about personal commitment.

Tell It to Jesus (page 150)

Not many hymn writers and composers have pseudonyms, but the author of "Tell It to Jesus" had more than one variation on his name. Edmund S. Lorenz was also known as E.D. Mund and L.S. Edwards. Name changes were due, in part, to his family's immigration from Russia to the United States. Once in the United States, Lorenz moved several times; from Ohio to Pennsylvania to Connecticut. He also attended the University of Leipzig in Germany. Lorenz finally settled in Dayton, Ohio, where he served as pastor of the High Street United Brethren Church and wrote this hymn, along with several other compositions in the 1870s and 1880s.

A *call and response* song is one in which a soloist sings a musical phrase and the group answers in response. Here's an idea for the performance of this favorite old hymn. Have a soloist sing the question as in the first verse, "Are you weary, are you heavy-hearted?" Then the group can answer, "Tell it to Jesus, Tell it to Jesus." You could even use different soloists for each verse and spread the fun around. Use the standard ending by repeating the last phrase to give the song more finality as it closes. This is in a friendly key with only one sharp, so pianists should be in good shape.

Tell Me the Stories of Jesus (page 152)

Some confuse this hymn with "Tell It to Jesus," but the two songs have no connection. They were both written in the late 19th century, but an ocean separates their places of origin. William H. Parker wrote "Tell Me the Stories of Jesus" in Nottingham, England in 1885. He worked as an insurance agent but was active at the Chelsea Street Baptist Church. As a children's Sunday School teacher, he wrote the words for his young students to recite for the congregation. In 1903, 18 years later, Frederick A. Challinor wrote the tune for a competition sponsored by the National Sunday School Union in London. The hymn remains a favorite for children's choirs and gospel sing-alongs.

This song is arranged more fully than most of the hymns in this collection. It is simply written and has a nice, flowing left-hand part that keeps the song moving along. This tune is often used at Palm Sunday services, and is also a charming song for a children's group to sing. This version presents the first two verses in Bb major then *modulates,* changing keys to C. That's good for the pianist since C is an easier key than Bb. The piano part for the third verse isn't exactly the same as for verses one and two, so be ready to play something new. Play all three verses on this hymn because it tells a story. Keep it smooth and hold back on the tempo.

Thine Is the Glory (page 158)

In 1824, Ludwig van Beethoven stated, "Handel is the greatest composer who ever lived. I would bare my head and kneel at his grave." George Frideric Handel could receive no greater compliment. Although Beethoven is arguably the Babe Ruth of classical music, Handel certainly played in the big leagues. He was born in Germany, educated in Italy, and lived most of his life in England. His reputation as a composer in the Baroque period is unsurpassed. Handel's most famous work is the *Messiah;* in fact, many refer to it as *Handel's Messiah.* Edmond L. Budry wrote the lyrics for the hymn "Thine Is the Glory" in 1884. However, it is Handel's composition *Judas Maccabaeus* (where this tune originated) that truly resonates with choirs and congregations as they sing this hymn.

This hymn tune is big-sounding and celebratory, and is usually heard during the Easter season. Keep it big and *majestic,* which means at a full volume and with a moderately slow tempo. The left hand of this arrangement has a lot of octaves, many of them moving along as eighth notes. If you have problems with those passages, just play the lower octave note. You'll lose a little of the power, but right notes are more important than the extra note of that octave. To emphasize the statement of victory at the end, a *ritard,* or slowing down, is appropriate each time with a return to the majestic tempo on the repeat. To give the voices a little rest, you could restate the introduction between verses two and three. Repeating left hand notes on the written whole notes, with quarter notes at the end of the phrase each time will keep a majestic march-feel going.

This Little Light of Mine *(page 155)*

"This Little Light of Mine" remains a children's classic, complete with hand motions and a catchy chorus. Many assume that the tune began as an African-American spiritual, but no evidence has been found to support this claim. More likely, Harry Loes wrote the song around 1920. Loes studied with Dwight L. Moody, the famous evangelist and educator. Zilphia Horton and Fannie Lou Hamer helped make this gospel song an anthem of the Civil Rights movement in the 1950s and 1960s. Other anthems of the period include "We Shall Overcome," "We Shall Not Be Moved," and "Go, Tell It on the Mountain." Fannie Lou Hamer was instrumental in the Student Nonviolent Coordinating Committee (SNCC) and the Democratic Party. She was straightforward, passionate, deeply spiritual, and a dynamic speaker. It was Hamer who first spoke the now common phrase "I am sick and tired of being sick and tired." *The Washington Post* wrote, "One is forced to pause and consider that this black daughter of the Old South might have been braver than King and Malcolm." Fittingly, the biography of her life, released in 2007 by author Kay Mills, is entitled "This Little Light of Mine."

If there ever was a *toe-tapper* in the hymn field, this is it. With a definite *shuffle* feel, it needs a strong bass line in a two beat per bar style. The melody is *syncopated,* which means there are accents off the beat, but that won't be a problem with this swinging little tune. Here's the road map for this tune: Start at the beginning, sing and play down to the third page where it says *D.S. al Coda.* That means go back to the sign (𝄋) and sing to the *To Coda* direction. When you get there, jump to the *Coda* at the end. Good luck and try not to get lost; there's no place to stop for directions. Feel free to extend the ending by repeating the line, "Gonna let my little light shine," a couple of extra times. Singers will have fun embellishing the melody on this popular song.

Wayfaring Stranger *(page 160)*

The source of this song is unknown. Hymnologists and historians disagree, but fragmented evidence exists to support multiple claims of origin including Appalachian folk, Irish folk, and African-American spirituals. Most likely, "Wayfaring Stranger" is influenced by all three musical cultures. This hymn became one of Burl Ives' signature songs. Ives recorded an album in 1944 entitled *The Wayfaring Stranger,* and it was also the title of his autobiography. Ives hosted a CBS radio show in the 1940s. In the 1960s he began recording as a country singer. In addition to his success in music and broadcasting, Ives also co-starred in *Cat on a Hot Tin Roof, The Big Country,* and *The Spiral Road.* However, he is best remembered as the voice of "Sam the Snowman" in the clay animation masterpiece *Rudolph the Red-Nosed Reindeer.* As for "Wayfaring Stranger," another interesting story lurks behind the music. Just as Charles D. Tillman claimed the rights to "Give Me That Old Time Religion," he also first published and popularized, "I Am a Poor Wayfaring Stranger." Tillman published the song in his 1891 compilation entitled *Revival.* Tillman had a knack for obtaining great music and finding a way to gain notoriety from previously unpublished folk songs and spirituals.

Of all the sad folk songs, this may be of the saddest of them all. Naturally, the tempo is a slow one. Make the *fermata* in the second full measure optional. You might just want to observe it on the first verse only for effect. Because there is no written introduction in this arrangement, try setting the mood and tempo with repeated C minor triads, or simple C, E♭, and G chords in the right hand and a sustained C in the left hand. That would also be a good interlude between verses to set them apart and allow whoever is singing a chance to rest a bit. The usual repeat of the last phrase, "I am just going over home," with a *decrescendo* and *ritard* closes out this morose melody and text.

We Are Climbing Jacob's Ladder (page 162)

This hymn represents a parallel between the Biblical struggle of the Jews and the historical struggle of African-American slaves. The Jewish patriarch Jacob dreamed that he stood in front of a ladder that connected heaven and earth. God spoke to Jacob and said, "Behold, I am with you and will keep you wherever you go, and will bring you back to this land; for I will not leave you until I have done that of which I have spoken to you." God's covenant led Jacob, and he named the town Bethel, which translates "House of God." The song developed in the United States first as a spiritual but is also considered a gospel hymn, children's chorus, and folk song.

You can approach the performance of this hymn in several ways. The arrangement here is in a reflective, easy three, with *shuffle-feel* eighth notes. Each verse should grow in intensity and dynamics to keep the momentum of the song moving forward. There's even a nice ending written for the final verse. Another approach is to perform the song in a 4/4 feel by adding a beat and increasing the tempo of the song. This makes the song more of a celebrative experience than a reflective one. Either style is fine; in fact, you can adapt this song to be appropriate to the context of its performance.

We Gather Together (page 164)

This hymn has endured several translations, first from Dutch to Latin and then from German to English. It was originally written as a praise song in 1597 to celebrate the Dutch victory against the Spanish in the Battle of Turnhout. The battle occurred as part of the Eighty Years' War, and Turnhout was a strategic border town area that separated North and South Netherlands. The Eighty Years' War is also known as the Dutch War of Independence, when Netherlanders revolted against the rule of King Phillip II. The hymn first appeared in *Nederlandtsche Gedenckclanck* (translated *Dutch Remembrance Tunes*) in 1626. Adrianus Valerius wrote this and many more religious texts. He was also part of the Rederijkerskamer (translated Chamber of Eloquent Speakers), an amateur poets society in Veere. The hymn grew popular in the United States at the turn of the 20th century. This tune has become the nationally recognized "Thanksgiving anthem" so it's a good one to have under your fingers, even though its usage is limited to just a couple of days a year.

In this arrangement, the left-hand part is quite active with some wide leaps. If things get too busy or too spread out, just play the first note in the measure and sustain it throughout the bar. The right hand can carry the song. The introduction works as an interlude if you need one between verses two and three. The *tessitura,* or overall range, of this song is on the high side, so if you have singers, give them plenty of full support. If you have the skills, you can play this song in D♭ major by just playing it in five flats rather than two sharps. That relieves some of the high notes for the singers. It's a good group song, so be thankful for it.

Were You There? (page 166)

Many slaves in the 18th and 19th centuries endured violence at the hands of their masters or were even murdered. According to Robert Darden, author of *People Get Ready: A New History of Black Gospel Music,* "To African-Americans, to be unjustly accused and nonchalantly killed was an all-too-regular occurrence." As such, several spirituals touch upon the theme of Jesus' torture and crucifixion. One such song was entitled "He Never Said a Mumblin' Word" to emphasize the silence and acceptance of Jesus as he endured his crucifixion. However, the hymn "Were You There?" remains the most well-known spiritual that deals with the crucifixion. It contains simple yet powerful lyrics. The song references his death on a "tree" throughout the hymn, which also provided vivid imagery for slaves, because family members were often hung or lynched in trees when murdered. This hymn, like many slave spirituals, contained many coded messages.

One of the most somber hymns in all of hymnody, each verse of this song describes an element of the crucifixion scene. Even though it is in a major key, the texture is dark and foreboding. Obviously, keep the tempo slow and plodding. In the last verse, try substituting the line "Were you there when He rose up from the grave?" It will be easy to do since it is repeated several times. You could pick up the tempo a little and brighten the ending on the final verse with a positive message of resurrection after the serious and ominous verses that comprise the rest of the song.

What a Friend We Have in Jesus (page 170)

This humble hymn also had humble beginnings. Joseph Scriven was in Dublin, Ireland in 1820. A graduate of Trinity College, Scriven planned to marry and start a family. The night before the wedding, tragedy struck. His fiancée was found dead in a pool of water and the case was ruled an accidental death. Scriven was devastated and moved to Canada in hopes of starting anew. The experience also led him to give up all of his material possessions. In Canada, he became a handyman and carpenter but only worked for, and with, the poor. In fact, he refused any job where there was a promise of pay. In 1857, a visiting neighbor happened upon a piece of paper. On it Scriven had written a poem and told the friend, "The Lord and I wrote it between us." The poem ultimately became the popular hymn "What a Friend We Have in Jesus." In 1869, Scriven published a collection of poems entitled *Hymns and Other Verses.* Sadly, in 1886, another body was pulled from the water — many of the citizens in Port Hope, Ontario believed that Joseph Scriven had taken his own life. A monument still stands in Port Hope, dedicated to the man who helped so many.

This hymn tune is well-known across the spectrum of denominations and styles of worship. As a result, the performance can be very straightforward, swinging, or even have a rock feel. This arrangement is well-written with a nice little rocking bass in the left hand to keep the movement going. One suggestion for pianists with smaller hands or less experience is to leave out the lower octaves, as in the first measure of the song when the lyrics start, and other places. You really won't miss them and it will be easier to finger the passages. The best tag if you want to expand the song is to repeat the final line, "In His arms He'll take and shield thee, thou wilt find a solace there." The language is rather Old English in this song, but folks are very familiar with it. (A lot of kids growing up thought that line was "Thou wilt find a *shoelace* there.")

When the Saints Go Marching In (page 172)

Louis Armstrong, the legendary jazz trumpeter and singer, recorded the most well-known version of this song. It seems only fitting. New Orleans is known as the home of jazz, and they have many "saintly" references. Saints figure prominently in this port city's history. New Orleans was founded as a French colony and remained a predominately Catholic community. Even their football team is named the New Orleans Saints. "When the Saints Go Marching In" also remains a traditional funeral hymn in the "Big Easy." Although the spiritual is a jazz standard, its use isn't limited to jazz. The hymn has been recorded in many genres including folk, rock, and religious. Luther G. Presley (no relation to Elvis), Judy Garland, Elvis Presley, Jerry Lee Lewis, Fats Domino, and Dolly Parton have all recorded this hymn. The song was first popularized in the 1930s, but the spiritual can be traced back to the 1870s. The words are apocalyptic and refer to the "Last Judgment" in the Book of Revelation.

Although the usual performance of this song is generally up-tempo in a celebrative Dixieland style, here's an idea that will create a little more interest and suspense. Start the introduction slowly with a free rhythm feel. Have a soloist sing the first verse in a slow tempo with any embellishments that come to mind, all the way down to the first ending. At the end of the first ending, kick it up a couple of notches in a bright march tempo on the lyric for the second verse, "Oh, when the sun..." Another idea to add to the building energy is to have a soloist sing an improvised echo to the last verse, with a group singing the main melody. Then add an ending of "When the saints go marching in," with a big slowdown for dramatic effect.

Wonderful Grace of Jesus (page 174)

The year 1918 was an important year. World War I, or The Great War, ended in Europe, and the United States helped secure an Allied victory against Germany. Author and composer Haldor Lillenas was well aware of the historical importance of 1918 and perhaps had that in mind when he wrote the hymn. Lillenas emigrated with his family from Norway to the United States. He lived in South Dakota, Oregon, California, Illinois, Indiana, Colorado, and Missouri. As he literally moved about the country, he gained the reputation of a passionate evangelist and musician. In 1924, he founded the Lillenas Music Company, which merged with the Nazarene Publishing Company in 1930. Lillenas wrote over 4,000 hymns during his lifetime. The Nazarene Publishing Company remains the main publisher for the Church of the Nazarene today, printing more than 25 million materials per year.

This song is one of the most rousing tunes in the hymn literature. It is a favorite at homecomings, revivals, and camp meetings, or wherever there is a joyous gathering of like-minded church folks. Fortunately, this arrangement is in C major rather than the original Db major. Not only is it easier to play, but it is not so high for the singers. Playing quarter notes in the left hand instead of just half notes is a good way to keep the rhythmic drive going. Another option is to sing a high G on the word "praise" in the measure before the first ending. If a singer feels strong, go for it, along with a big *allargando*, which means slowing down and getting louder. Because the song is demanding on the voice, repeating the introduction for verse two gives the singer a chance to recover before the second verse.

Just as I Am

Words by Charlotte Elliott
Music by William B. Bradbury

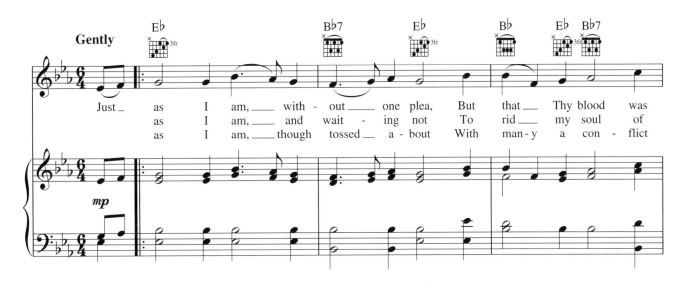

Just _ as I am, ___ with - out ___ one plea, But that ___ Thy blood was
as I am, ___ and wait - ing not To rid ___ my soul of
as I am, ___ though tossed ___ a - bout With man - y a con - flict

shed for me. And _ that Thou bidd'st ___ me come to Thee, ___ O
one dark blot, To _ Thee whose blood ___ can cleanse each spot. ___ O
many a doubt, Fight - ings and fears ___ with - in, with - out ___ O

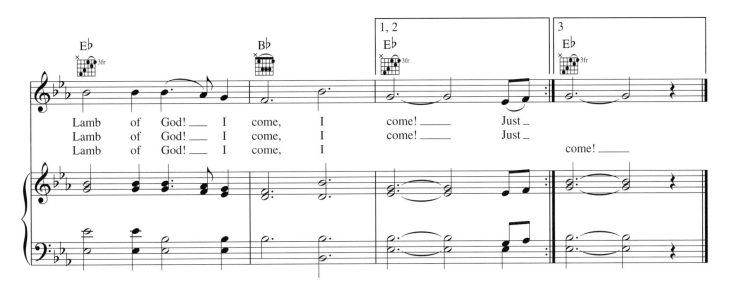

Lamb of God! ___ I come, I come! ____ Just _
Lamb of God! ___ I come, I come! ____ Just _
Lamb of God! ___ I come, I come! ____ come! ____

Kum Ba Yah

Traditional Spiritual

Lyrics (first staff system):
Kum ba yah, my Lord, Kum ba yah! Kum ba yah, my Lord, Kum ba
cry - in', Lord, Kum ba yah! Some-one's cry - in', Lord, Kum ba

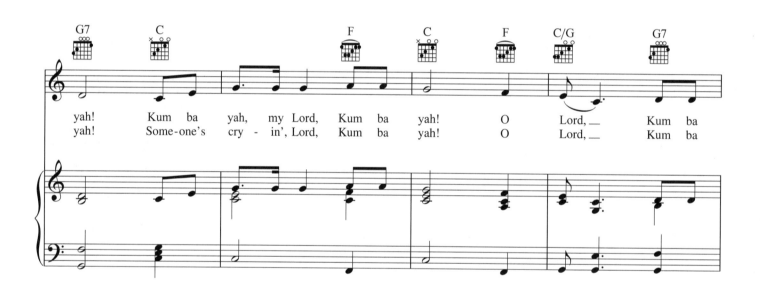

Lyrics (second staff system):
yah! Kum ba yah, my Lord, Kum ba yah! O Lord, — Kum ba
yah! Some-one's cry - in', Lord, Kum ba yah! O Lord, — Kum ba

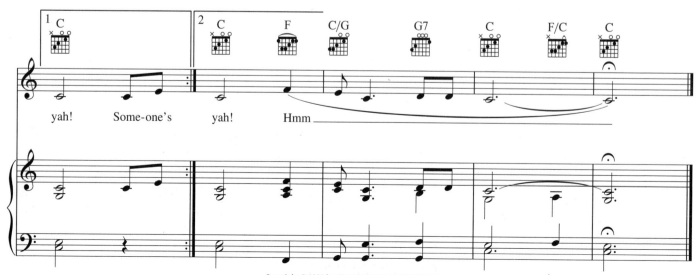

Lyrics (third staff system):
yah! Some-one's yah! Hmm _____

Lift Ev'ry Voice and Sing

Words by James Weldon Johnson
Music by J. Rosamond Johnson

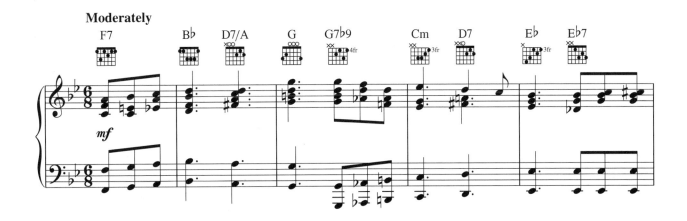

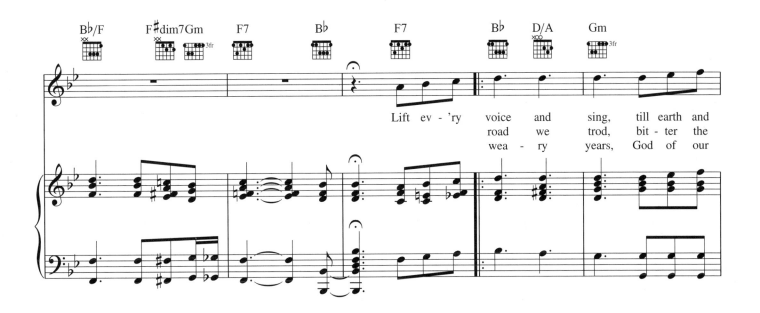

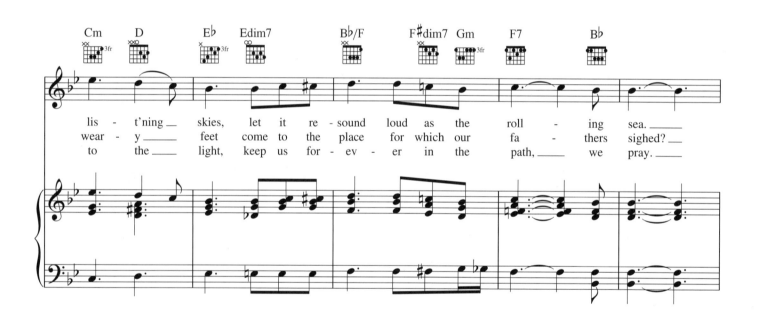

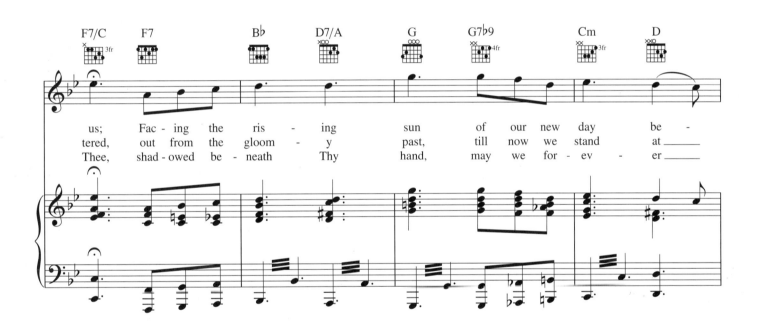

Leaning on the Everlasting Arms

Words by Elisha A. Hoffman
Music by Anthony J. Showalter

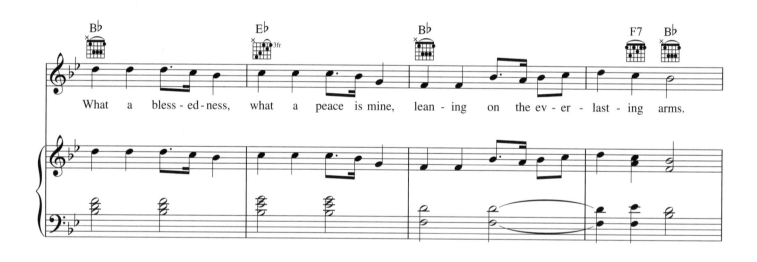

The Lord Bless You and Keep You

Words and Music by Peter C. Lutkin

The Lord's My Shepherd, I'll Not Want

Words from *Scottish Psalter,* 1650
Based on Psalm 23
Music by Jessie S. Irvine

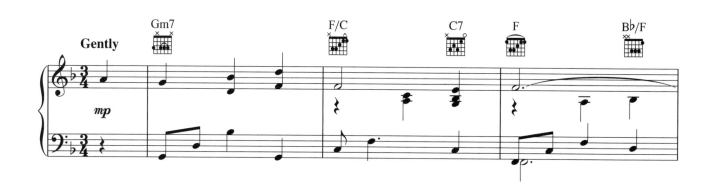

The   Lord's   my ____ Shep -   herd; ____
soul   though   I ____ walk   Thou   hast ____
ta -   ble   and ____ mer   -   cy ____
ness

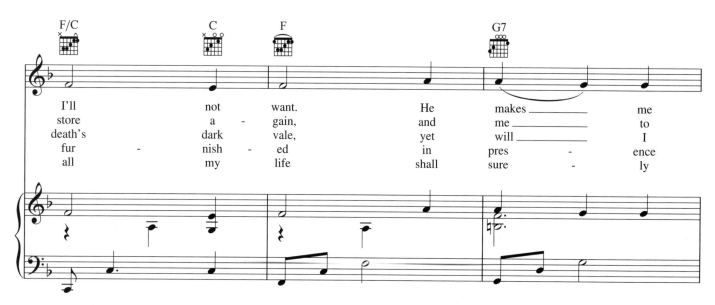

I'll   not   want.   He   makes _____ me
store   a -   gain,   and   me _____ to
death's   dark   vale,   yet   will _____ I
fur -   nish - ed   life   in   pres   -   ence
all   my   shall   sure   -   ly

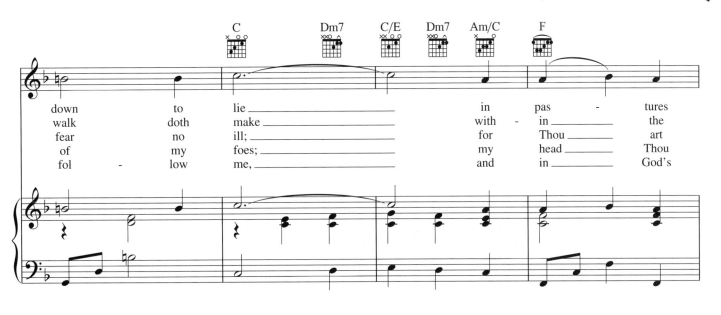

Love Lifted Me

Words by James Rowe
Music by Howard E. Smith

Moderately fast

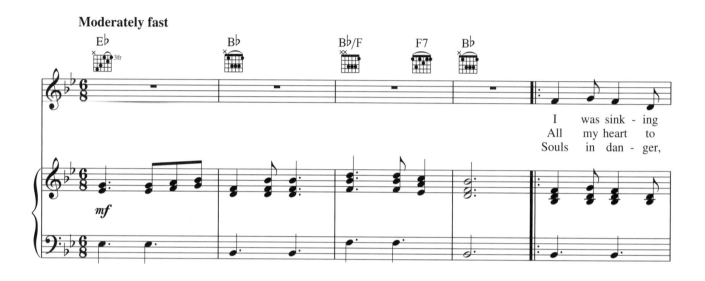

I was sink - ing
All my heart to
Souls in dan - ger,

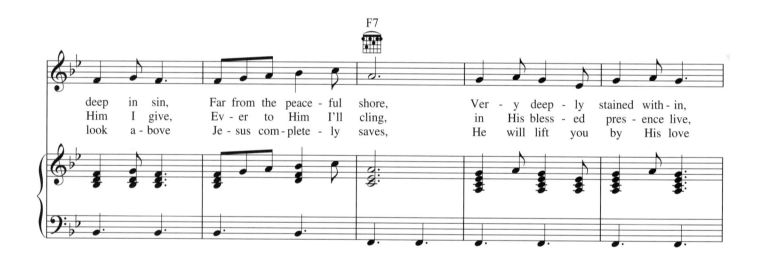

deep in sin, Far from the peace - ful shore, Ver - y deep - ly stained with - in,
Him I give, Ev - er to Him I'll cling, in His bless - ed pres - ence live,
look a - bove Je - sus com - plete - ly saves, He will lift you by His love

Sink - ing to rise no more; but the Mas - ter of the sea Heard my de - spair - ing
ev - er His prais - es sing; Love so might - y and so true Mer - its my soul's best
Out of the an - gry waves; He's the Mas - ter of the sea, Bil - lows His will o -

A Mighty Fortress Is Our God

Words and Music by Martin Luther
Translated by Frederick H. Hedge
Based on Psalm 46

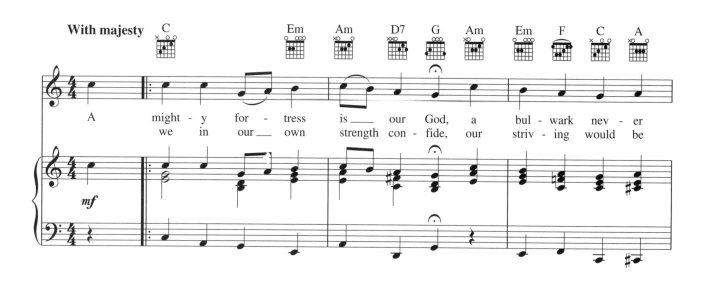

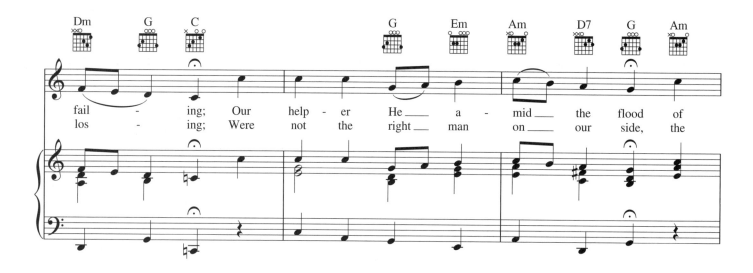

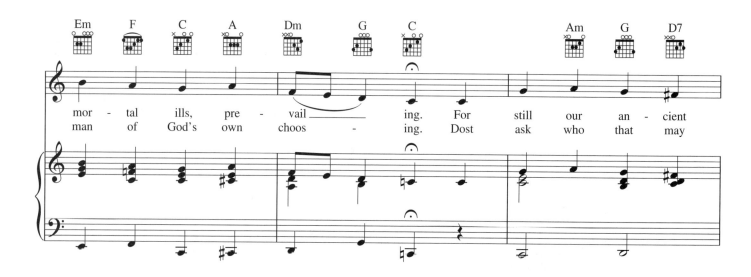

And tho this world, with devils filled,
Should threaten to undo us;
We will not fear, for God hath willed
His truth to triumph through us;
The Prince of darkness grim,
We tremble not for him;
His rage we can endure,
For lo! His doom is sure,
One little word shall fell him.

That word above all earthly powers,
No thanks to them abideth,
The spirit and the gifts are ours
Through Him who with us sideth;
Let goods and kindred go,
This mortal life also;
The body they may kill;
God's truth abideth still,
His kingdom is forever.

My Faith Looks Up to Thee

Words by Ray Palmer
Music by Lowell Mason

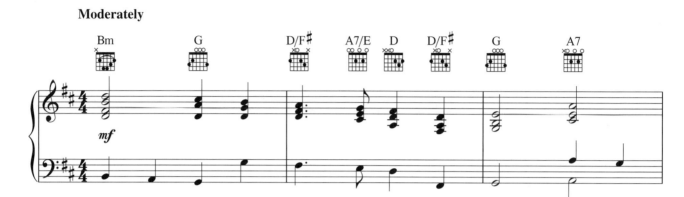

My   faith   looks   up   to   Thee,
May   Thy   rich   grace   im - part
While   life's   dark   maze   I   tread
When   ends   life's   pass - ing   dream,

Thou   Lamb   of   Cal -   va - ry,   Sav -   ior   di -
Strength   to   my   faint - ing   heart,   My   zeal   in -
And   griefs   a -   round   me   spread, Be   Thou   my
When   death's cold,   threat - 'ning stream Shall   o'er   me

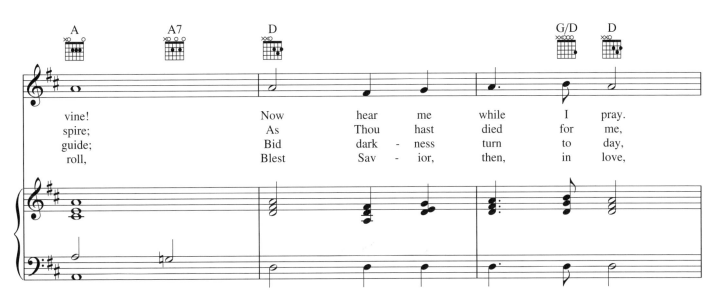

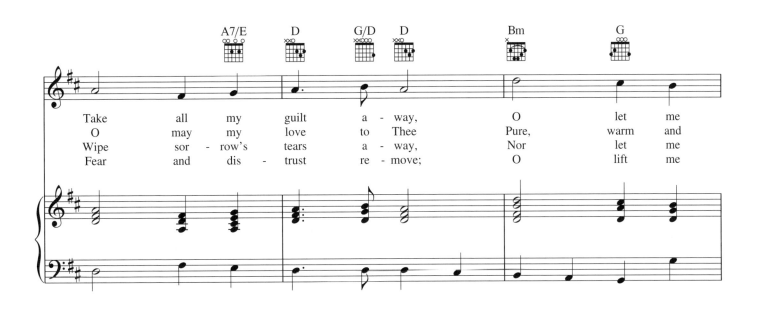

Nearer, My God, to Thee

Words by Sarah F. Adams
Based on Genesis 28:10-22
Music by Lowell Mason

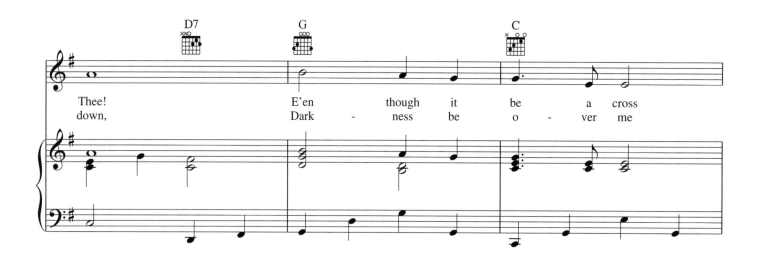

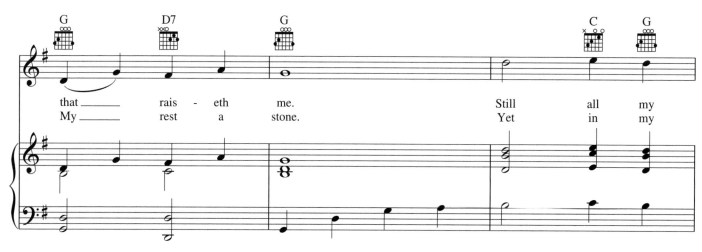

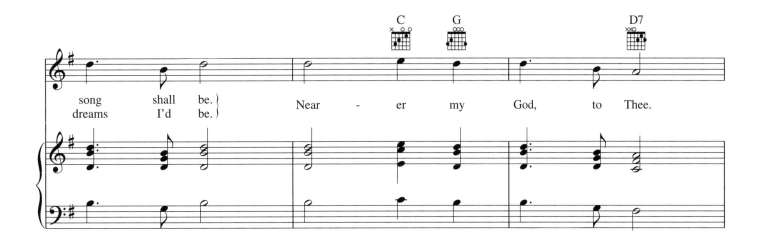

song   shall   be.   }   Near -   er   my   God,   to   Thee.
dreams   I'd   be. }

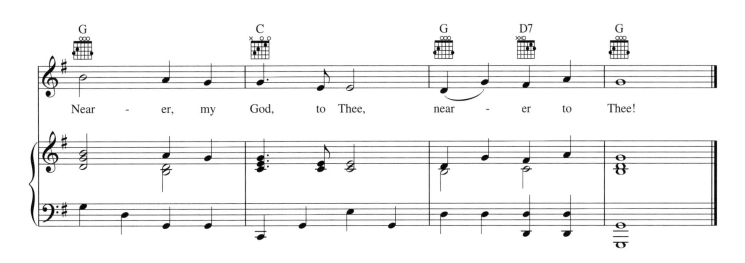

Near -   er,   my   God,   to   Thee,   near -   er   to   Thee!

Then with my waking thoughts
Bright with Thy praise,
Out of my stony griefs
Bethel I'll raise
So by my woes to be,
Nearer, my God, to Thee,
Nearer, my God, to Thee,
Nearer to Thee!

Or if on joyful wing,
Cleaving the sky,
Sun, moon, and stars forgot,
Upwards I'll fly.
Still all my song shall be,
Nearer, my God, to Thee,
Nearer, my God, to Thee,
Nearer to Thee!

O Perfect Love

Words by Dorothy Frances Gurney
Music by Joseph Barnby

The Old Rugged Cross

Words and Music by Rev. George Bennard

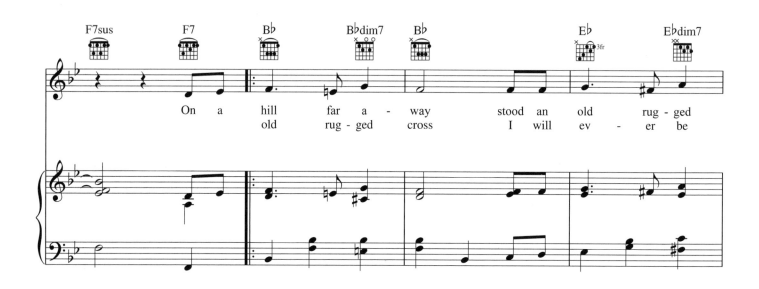

On a hill far a - way stood an old rug - ged
old rug - ged cross I will ev - er be

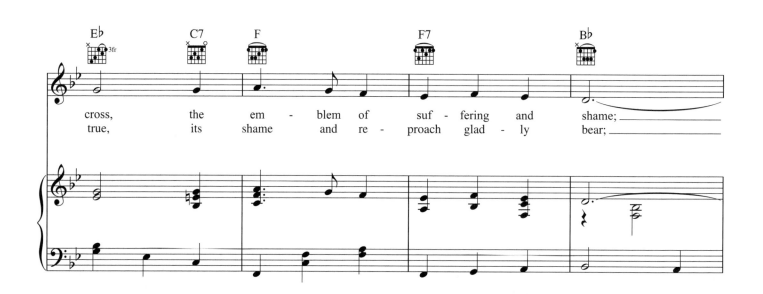

cross, the em - blem of suf - fering and shame;
true, its shame and re - proach glad - ly bear;

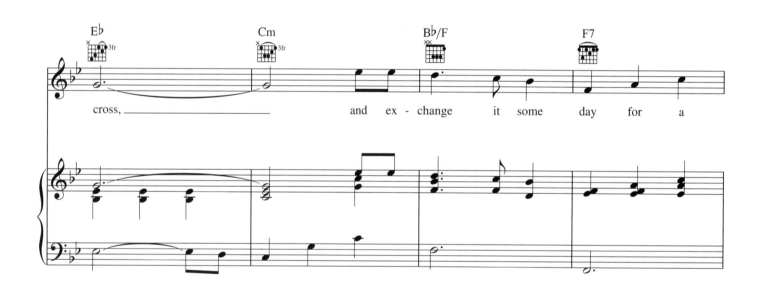

Onward, Christian Soldiers

Words by Sabine Baring-Gould
Music by Arthur S. Sullivan

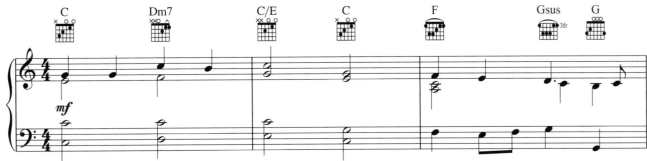

On - ward Chris - tian sol - - diers
Like a might - y ar - my
On - ward, then, ye peo - ple

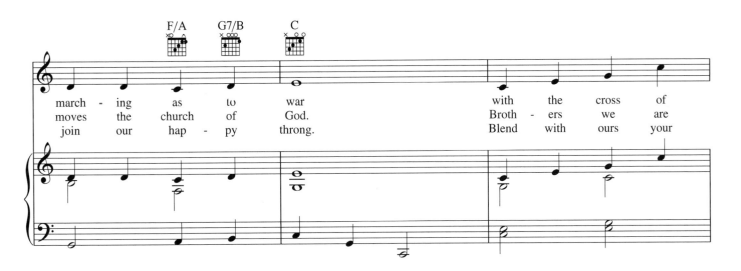

march - ing as to war
moves the church of God.
join our hap - py throng.

with the cross of
Broth - ers we are
Blend with ours your

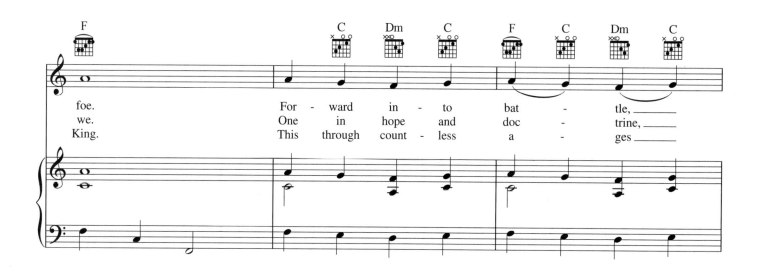

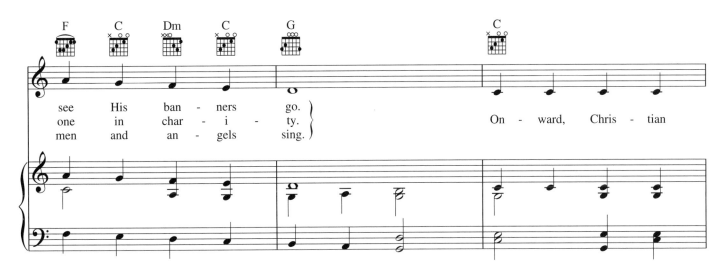

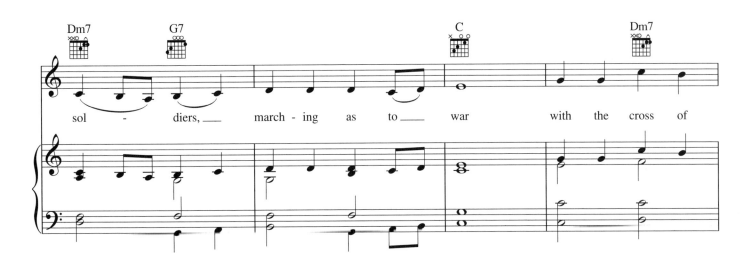

Only Trust Him

Words and Music by John H. Stockton

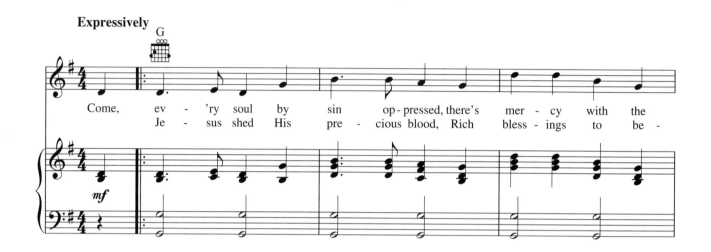

Come, ev-'ry soul by sin op-pressed, there's mer-cy with the
Je-sus shed His pre-cious blood, Rich bless-ings to be-

Lord. And He will sure-ly give you rest by
stow; Plunge now in-to the crim-son flood that

trust-ing in His word. }
wash-es white as snow. }

On-ly trust ___ Him,

on - ly trust Him, on - ly trust Him now.

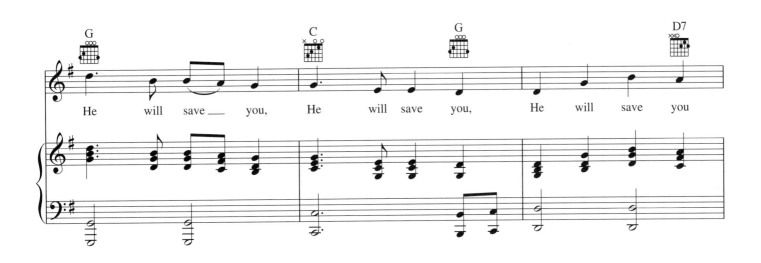

He will save ____ you, He will save you, He will save you

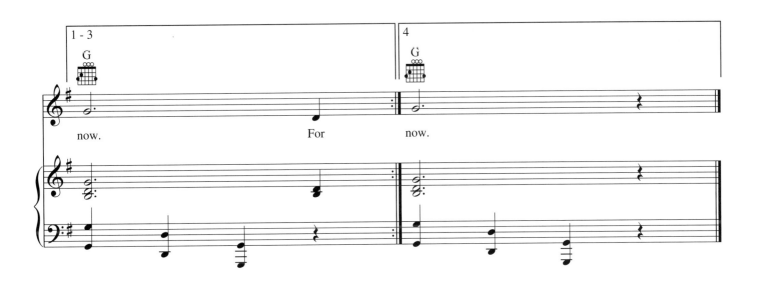

now.   For   now.

Yes, Jesus is the truth, the way,
That leads you into rest;
Believe in Him without delay,
And you are fully blest.

Come, then, and join this holy band,
And on to glory go,
To dwell in that celestial land.
Where joys immortal flow.

Precious Memories

Words and Music by J.B.F. Wright

Prayerfully

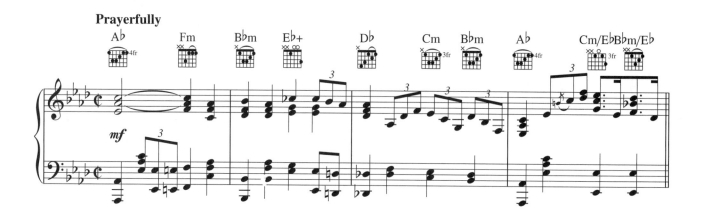

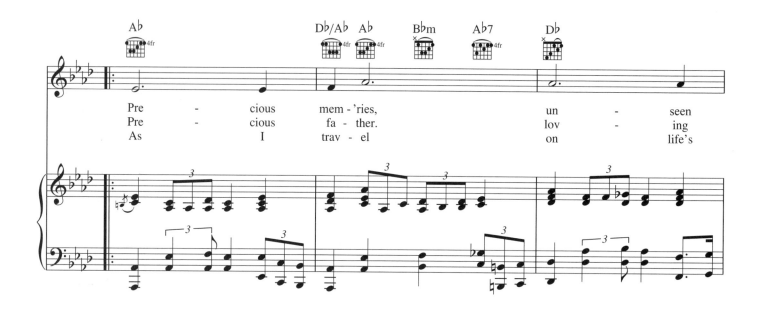

Pre - cious mem -'ries, un - seen
Pre - cious fa - ther. lov - ing
As I trav - el on life's

an - gels, Sent from ____ somewhere to my
moth - er, Fly a - cross the lone - ly
path - way, I know ____ not what life shall

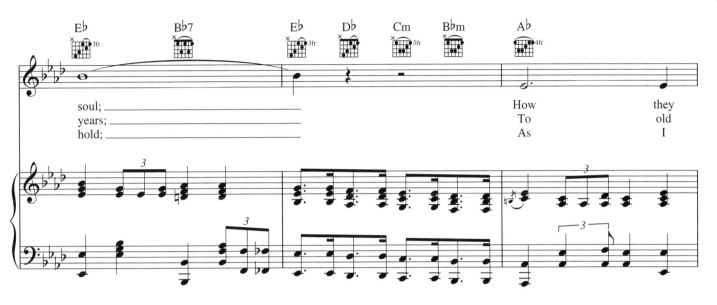

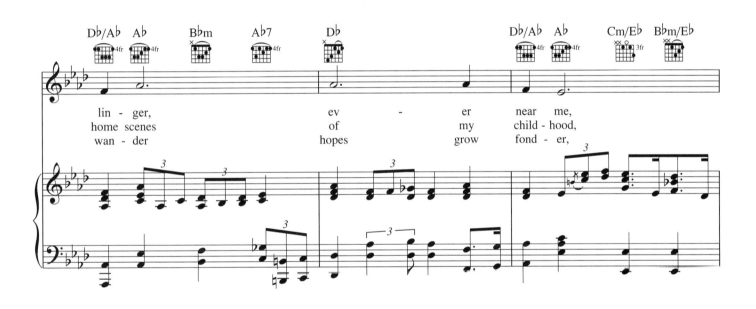

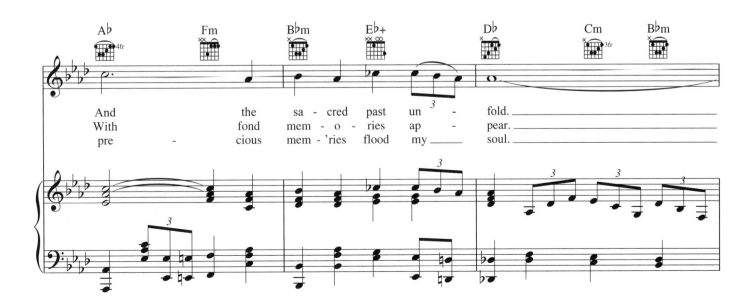

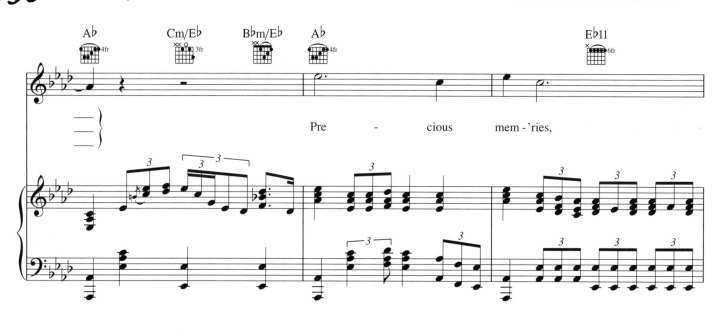

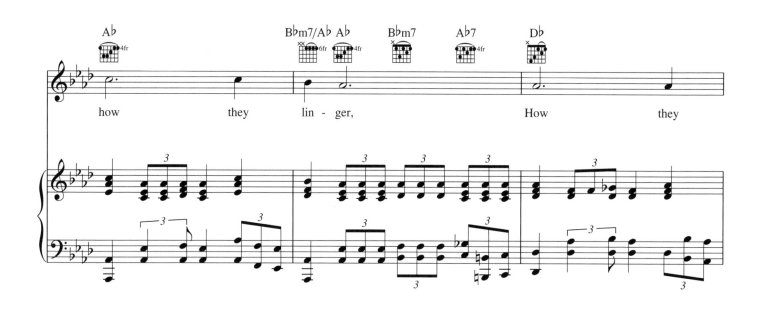

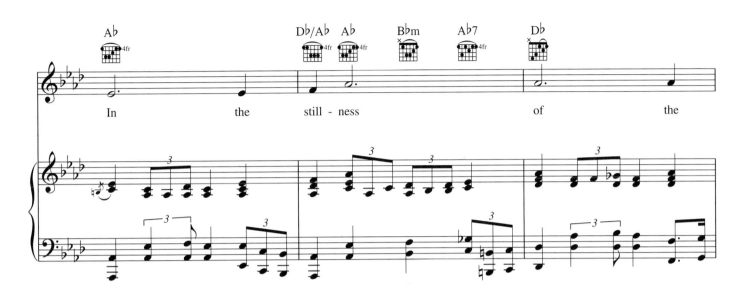

In the still - ness   of   the

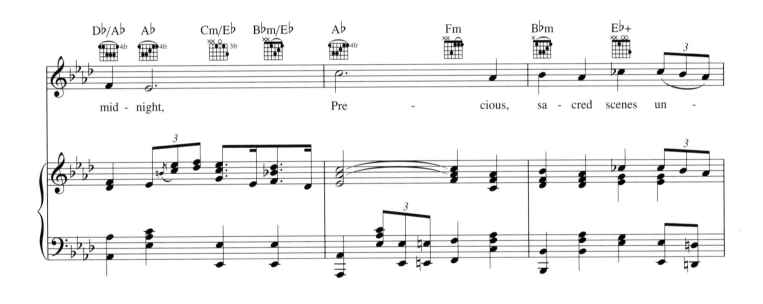

mid - night,   Pre   -   cious,   sa - cred scenes un -

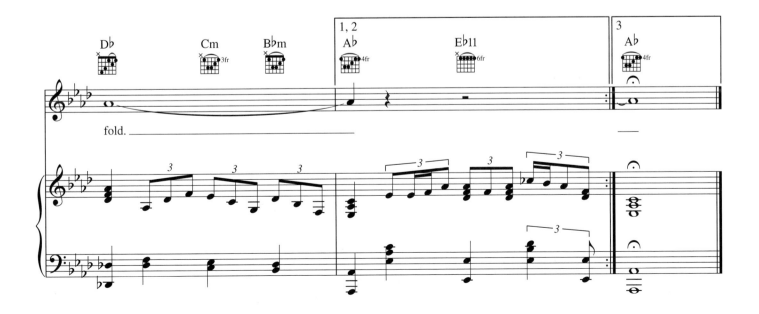

fold.

Rock of Ages

Words by Augustus M. Toplady
Music by Thomas Hastings

Take My Life and Let It Be

Words by Frances R. Havergal
Music by Henry A. César Malan

Simple Gifts

Traditional Shaker Hymn

Stand Up, Stand Up for Jesus

Words by George Duffield, Jr.
Music by George J. Webb

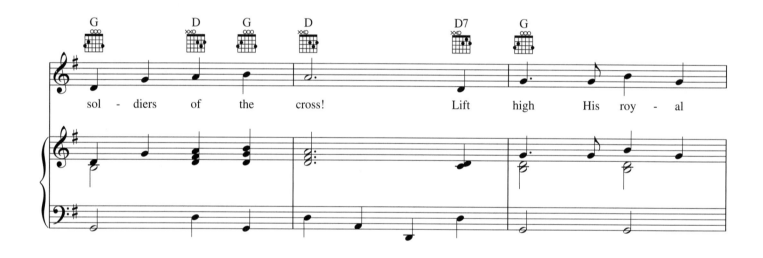

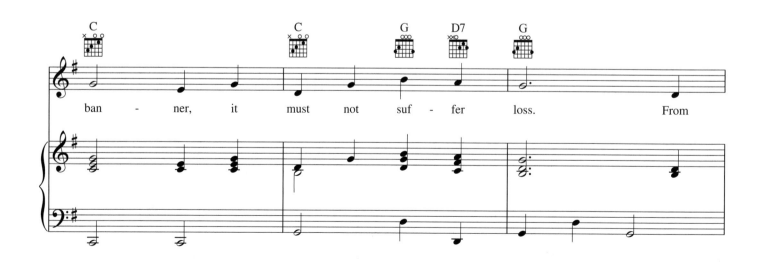

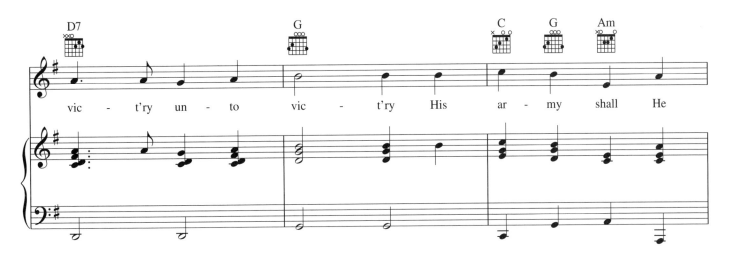

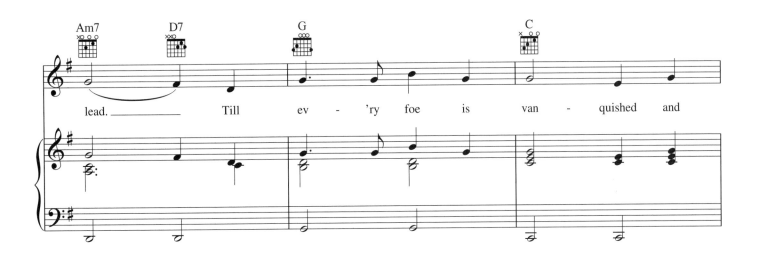

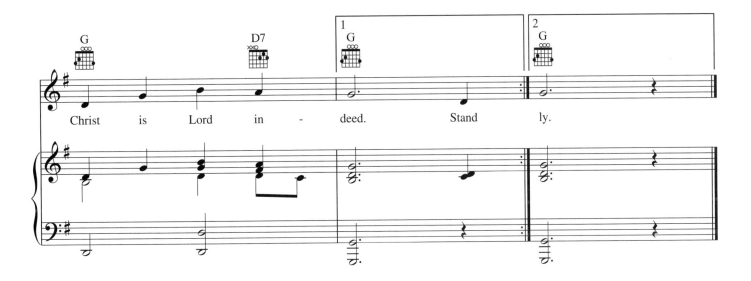

Stand up, stand up for Jesus,
The strife will not be long;
This day the noise of battle,
The next, the victor's song;
To him the overcometh,
A crown of life shall be;
He with the King of glory
Shall reign eternally.

Sweet By and By

Words by Sanford Fillmore Bennett
Music by Joseph P. Webster

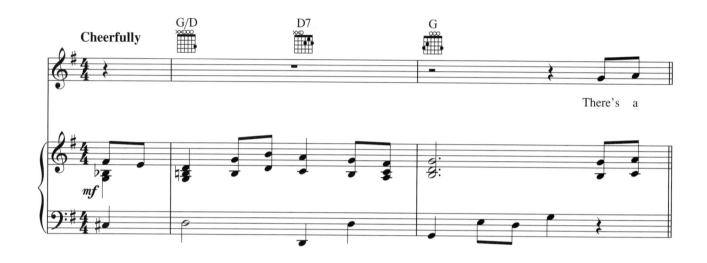

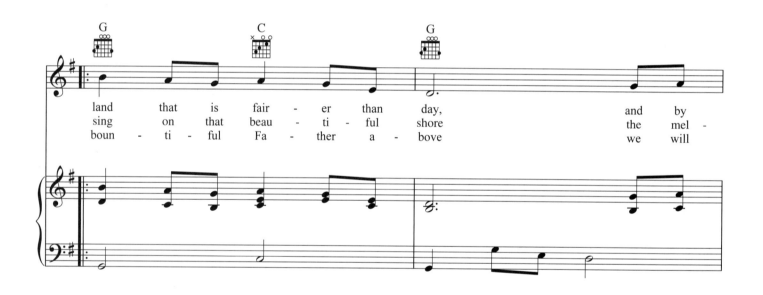

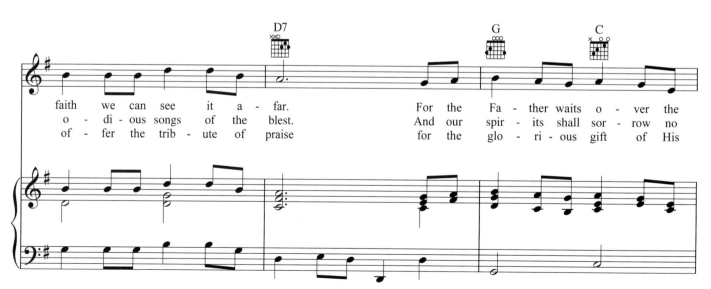

Sweet Hour of Prayer

Words by William W. Walford
Music by William B. Bradbury

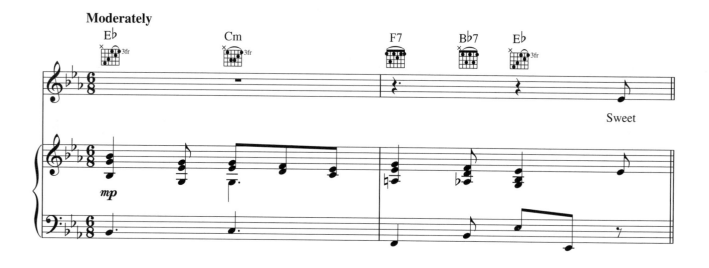

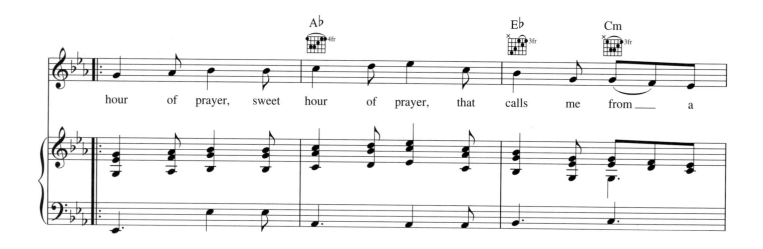

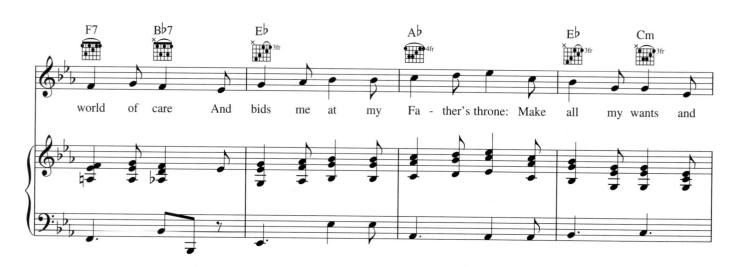

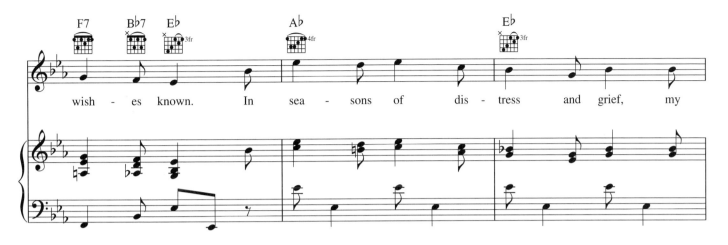

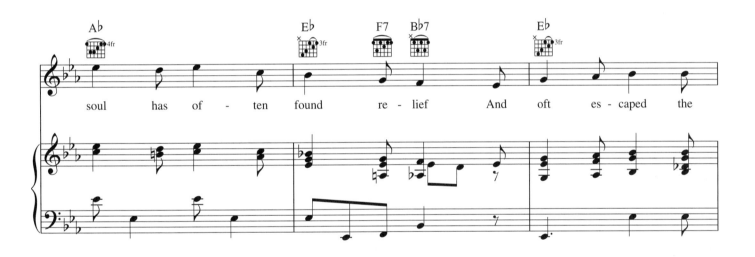

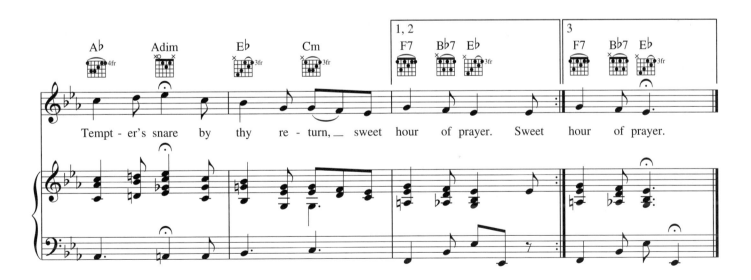

(Sweet) hour of prayer,
Sweet hour of prayer,
Thy wings shall my petition bear
To Him whose truth and faithfulness
Engage the waiting soul to bless.
And since He bids me seek His face,
Believe His word, and trust His grace,
I'll cast on Him my ev'ry care
And wait for thee, sweet hour of prayer.

(Sweet) hour of prayer,
Sweet hour of prayer,
May I thy consolation share
Till from Mount Pisgah's lofty height
I view my home and take my flight.
This robe of flesh I'll drop and rise
To seize the everlasting prize
And shout while passing through the air
Farewell, farewelll, sweet hour of prayer.

Tell It to Jesus

Words by Jeremiah E. Rankin
Music by Edmund S. Lorenz

Additional Verses

3. Do you fear the gath'ring clouds of sorrow?
   Tell it to Jesus, Tell it to Jesus;
   Are you anxious what shall be tomorrow?
   Tell it to Jesus alone.
   Refrain

4. Are you troubled at the thought of dying?
   Tell it to Jesus, Tell it to Jesus;
   For Christ's coming kingdom are you sighing?
   Tell it to Jesus alone.
   Refrain

Tell Me the Stories of Jesus

Words by William H. Parker
Music by Frederic A. Challinor

This Little Light of Mine

African-American Spiritual

Thine Is the Glory

Words by Edmond Louis Budry
Music by George Frideric Handel

Wayfaring Stranger

Southern American Folk Hymn

I am a poor way-far-ing stran-ger, While trav-'ling
sing Sal-va-tion's sto-ry in con-cert
free from ev-'ry tri-al, this form will

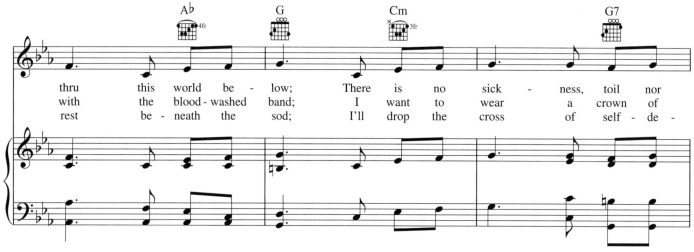

thru this world be-low; There is no sick-ness, toil nor
with the blood-washed band; I want to wear a crown of
rest be-neath the sod; I'll drop the cross of self-de-

dan-ger in that bright world to which I go. I'm go-ing
glo-ry, when I get home to that good land. I'm go-ing
ni-al, and en-ter in my home with God. I'm go-ing

there   to meet my   Fa - ther,   I'm go - ing   there   no more to
there   to meet the   saved ones   who passed be - fore   me one by
there   to see my   Sav - ior,   who shed for   me   His pre - cious

roam; }
one; }   I am just   go - ing o - ver   Jor - dan,   I am
blood; }

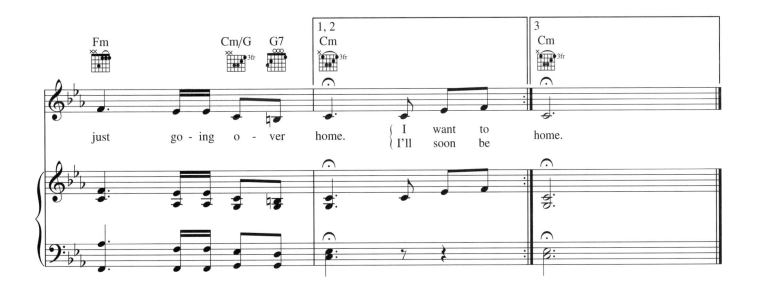

just   go - ing o - ver   home.   { I   want   to   home.
                                     { I'll   soon   be

We Are Climbing Jacob's Ladder

Traditional Spiritual

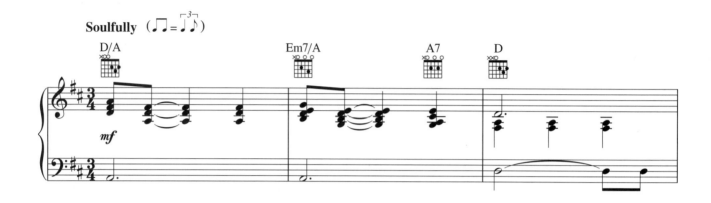

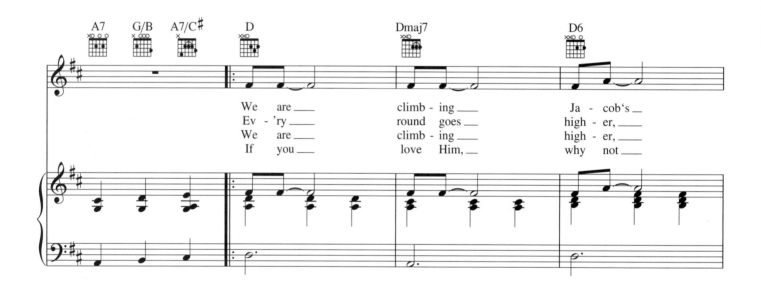

We are ____ climb - ing ____ Ja - cob's ____
Ev - 'ry ____ round goes ____ high - er, ____
We are ____ climb - ing ____ high - er, ____
If you ____ love Him, ____ why not ____

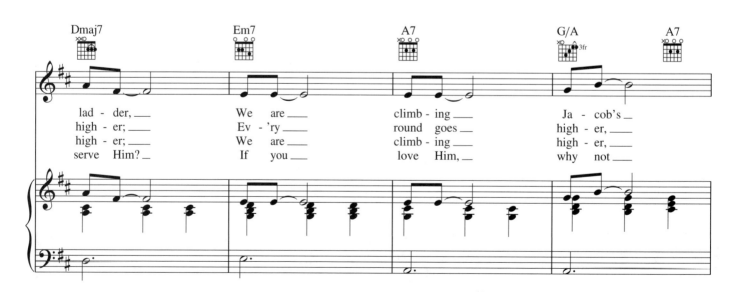

lad - der, ____ We are ____ climb - ing ____ Ja - cob's ____
high - er; ____ Ev - 'ry ____ round goes ____ high - er, ____
high - er; ____ We are ____ climb - ing ____ high - er, ____
serve Him? ____ If you ____ love Him, ____ why not ____

We Gather Together

Words from *Nederlandtsch Gedenckclanck*
Translated by Theodore Baker
Netherlands Folk Melody
Arranged by Edward Kremser

Were You There?

Traditional Spiritual
Harmony by Charles Winfred Douglas

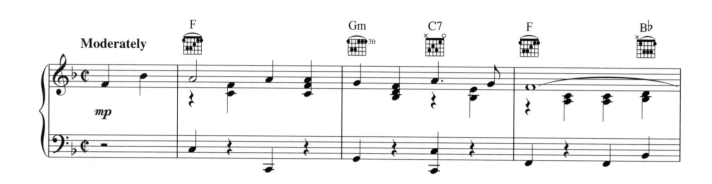

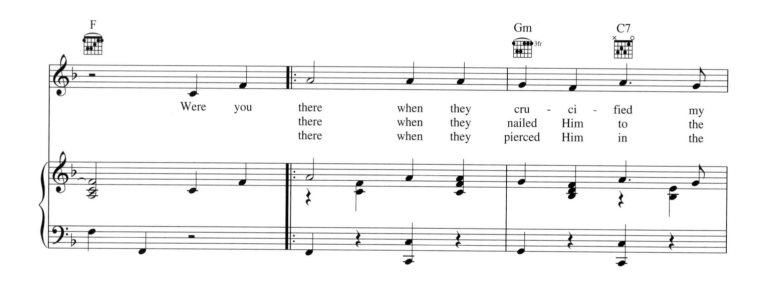

Were you there when they cru - ci - fied my
there when they nailed Him to the
there when they pierced Him in the

Lord? (Were you there?) Were you there when they
tree? Were you there when they
side? Were you there when they

cru - ci - fied my Lord? _____ Oh, _____
nailed Him to the tree? _____ Oh, _____
pierced Him in the side? _____ Oh, _____

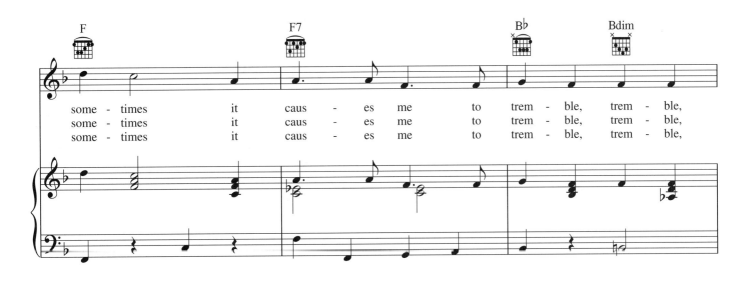

some - times it caus - es me to trem - ble, trem - ble,
some - times it caus - es me to trem - ble, trem - ble,
some - times it caus - es me to trem - ble, trem - ble,

trem - ble. Were you there when they cru - ci - fied my
trem - ble. Were you there when they nailed Him to the
trem - ble. Were you there when they pierced Him in the

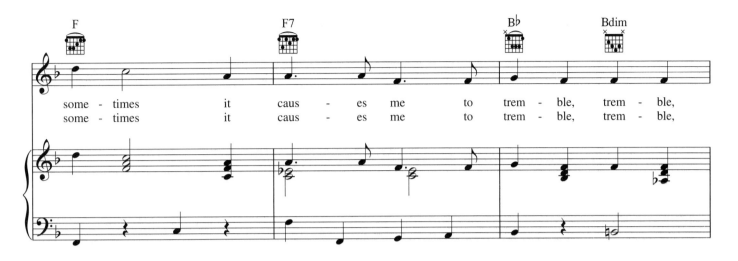

some - times it caus - es me to trem - ble, trem - ble,
some - times it caus - es me to trem - ble, trem - ble,

trem - ble. Were you there when the sun re - fused to
trem - ble. Were you there when they laid Him in to the

shine? _____ Were you tomb? _____
(Were you there?) (In the tomb?)

What a Friend We Have in Jesus

Words by Joseph M. Scriven
Music by Charles C. Converse

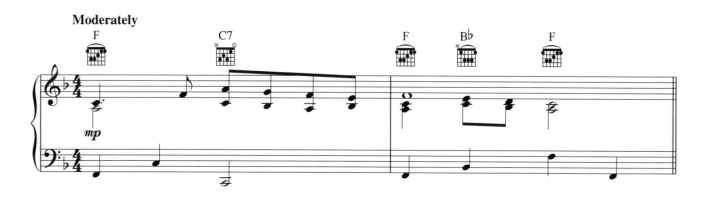

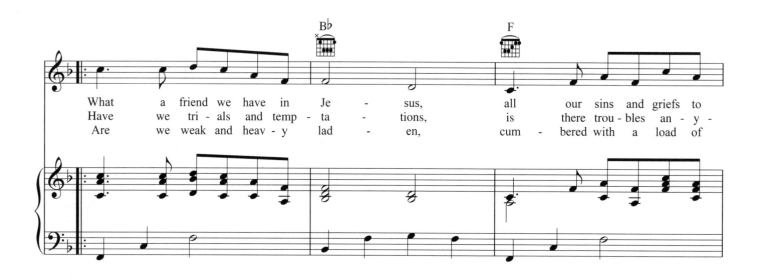

What a friend we have in Je - sus, all our sins and griefs to
Have we tri - als and temp - ta - tions, is there trou - bles an - y -
Are we weak and heav - y lad - en, cum - bered with a load of

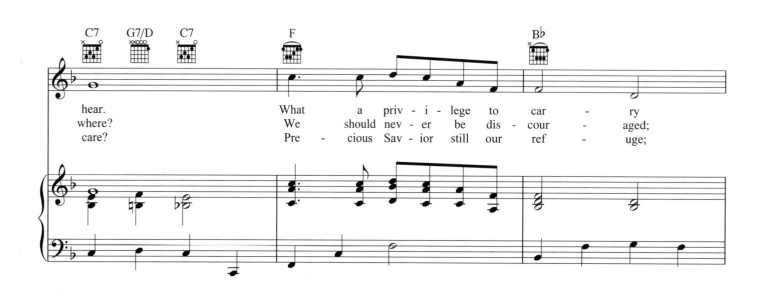

hear. What a priv - i - lege to car - ry
where? We should nev - er be dis - cour - aged;
care? Pre - cious Sav - ior still our ref - uge;

ev - 'ry - thing to God in prayer.   Oh,   what peace we of - ten
take   it to the Lord in prayer.   Can   we find a friend so
take   it to the Lord in prayer.   Do   thy friends de - spise, for -

for - feit,   oh, what need - less pain we bear,   all be - cause we do not
faith - ful   who will all our sor - rows share?   Je - sus knows our ev - 'ry
sake thee?   Take it to the Lord in prayer.   In His arms He'll take and

car - ry   ev - 'ry - thing to God in prayer.
weak - ness;   take it to the Lord in prayer.
shield thee;   thou will find a so - lace   there.

When the Saints Go Marching In

Words by Katherine E. Purvis
Music by James M. Black

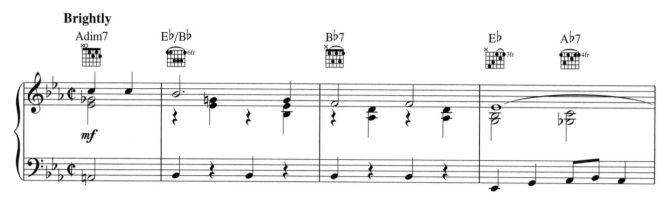

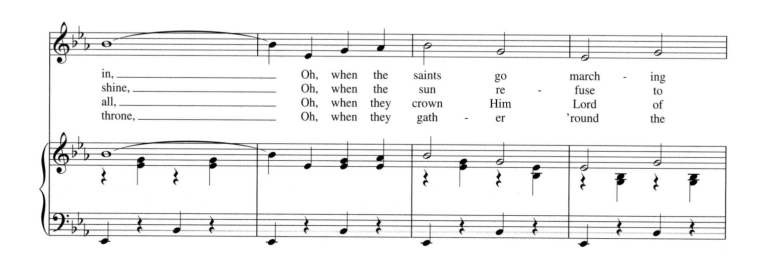

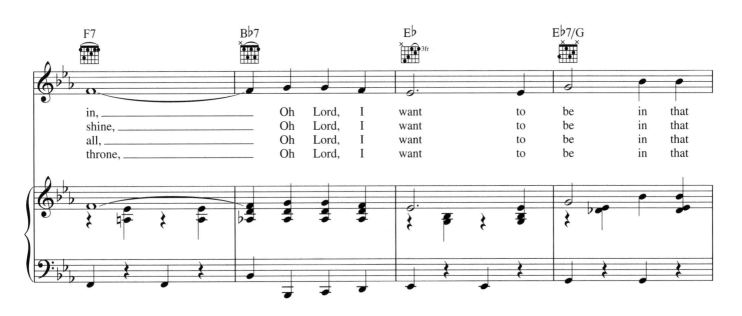

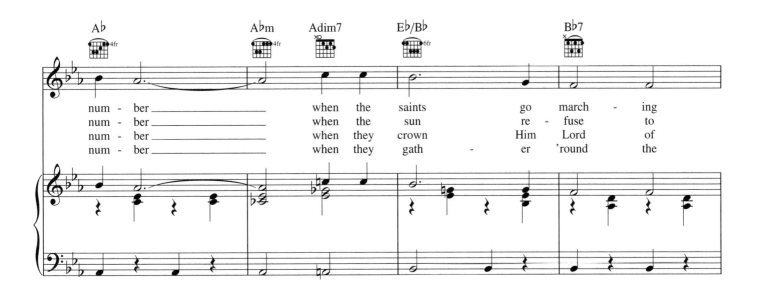

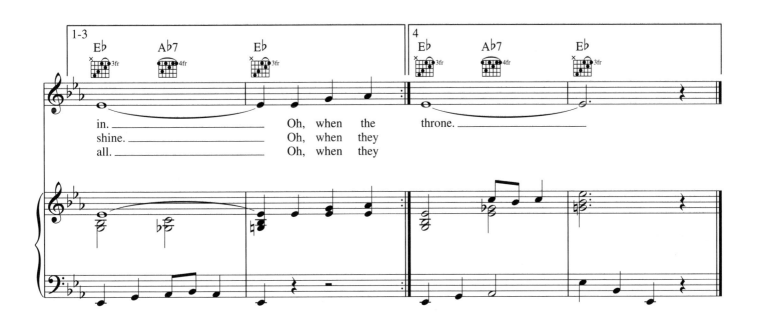

Wonderful Grace of Jesus

Words and Music by Haldor Lillenas